WEATHER Wise

Creative Activities About the Environment

by Robynne Eagan and
Tracey Ann Schofield

illustrated by Wendy Grieb

D1517582

Teaching & Learning Company

1204 Buchanan St., P.O. Box 10
Carthage, IL 62321-0010

This book belongs to

_____

Cover by Wendy Grieb

Back cover photo of Tracey Ann Schofield by Glamour Shots®

Copyright © 1997, Teaching & Learning Company

ISBN No. 1-57310-072-2

Printing No. 98765432

Teaching & Learning Company
1204 Buchanan St., P.O. Box 10
Carthage, IL 62321-0010

Dedication

For my children, my husband and my parents . . . they are my sunshine.
T.S.

To the four winds that blow, the rain and snow that falls, the sun that shines and the rainbows that arc across the sky.   R.E.

Acknowledgements

The authors would like to thank Denise Shannon and Sue Truong (meteorologist) for their assistance in putting this book together.

Table of Contents

TLC10072 Copyright © Teaching & Learning Company, Carthage, IL 62321-0010

Dear Teacher or Parent,

Mark Twain once said, "Everybody talks about the weather, but nobody does anything about it." He was right. Like it or not, we have little real influence over the weather we experience. It just happens.

While we might not be able to change the weather, however, we can learn to understand it. By reading, experimenting, observing and recording, we can find out about the causes and effects of weather and prepare ourselves in advance for both its good and bad results.

WEATHER Wise is a young student's introduction to weather. Intended as a resource tool for educators, *WEATHER Wise* offers 10 chapters of lively, easy-to-understand scientific explanations, hands-on learning tasks, classroom experiments, language and math activities, history and geography orientation lessons, bulletin board ideas, fun facts and folklore and creative arts suggestions. Chapters are organized by weather type, and this simple format enables educators to connect weather themes to all areas of the curriculum and opens the door to exciting learning discoveries.

WEATHER Wise offers educators a stimulating resource guide to using the environment to enhance a child's natural curiosity and foster creative learning. In-class discussions, activities and seatwork act as a springboard to further discoveries, and firsthand sensory experiences bring these lessons to life. The unique approach used in *WEATHER Wise* encourages children to formulate questions, investigate and make their own discoveries as they become "weather wise."

Sincerely,

Robynne   *Tracey*

Robynne Eagan and Tracey Ann Schofield

Symbols

Please take note of the following symbols for at-a-glance information regarding the various experiments:

 indoor activity

 outdoor activity

 warning, activity requires caution/adult intervention

 5 to 30-minute activity

 30 to 60-minute activity

 60+ minute activity

Curriculum Links

The information and activities in this book can be extended and incorporated into most curriculum areas to facilitate development of various skills. The following symbols will indicate which curriculum areas are specifically targeted through the activity.

 Language

 Science

 Geography

 Physical Education

 Music

 Math

 Art

 Design and Technology

 History

 Health

A Word About Experiments

Kids learn best with hands-on activity. Experiments in this book are designed to help kids learn about weather through active investigation. Simple procedures and the use of everyday materials make it easy for children to be actively involved throughout the learning process.

Establish rules for safety before conducting any experiment. Remind children to take care with all tools, equipment, sharp objects and glass.

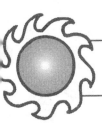

Chapter 1
What Is Weather?

We see and feel the weather as wind that blows our hair, as heat that warms our bodies, as cold that nips our nose and toes and as rain that soaks our skin. We see the weather in billowy clouds, blue skies and sunshine, frost on the ground, swirling snow and foggy days. From the hot, still days of summer to the wildest harsh storms of winter, weather is a fascinating part of our world.

To understand weather we look to the blanket of gases called the atmosphere that surrounds our Earth. The atmosphere is about 600 miles (1000 km) above you and is arranged in four layers. This atmosphere separates us from outer space and makes the Earth different from all other planets.

The layer closest to the Earth is 12 miles thick (19 km), weighs more than any other layer and supports all life on Earth. It is called the troposphere and contains the air we live in and breathe. Technically, weather is the condition of the troposphere. The sun's heat keeps the wind and water in the troposphere heating and swirling to give us our endless cycle of changing weather. Our rain, snow, sleet, hail, thunder, lightning and rainbows all happen here, in the troposphere.

The usual kind of weather that a particular place experiences over a long period of time is called its climate. People all over the world adapt to their particular climate. People's traditions, homes, foods, clothes, means of travel and day-to-day activities are adapted to reflect the kind of weather they experience.

Weather is fascinating and ever-changing, and it shapes our lives every day.

Air is all around us in the troposphere and without it there would be no people, plants or animals on Earth. We can swallow it, breathe it, move it and watch what it does, but we cannot see it. It consists of many invisible gases (mostly nitrogen and oxygen gases).

Weather Watch Symbols

Sunny

Showers

Fog

Thunderstorm

Rain

Cold Front

Warm Front

Snow

Cloudy

Partly Cloudy

Windy

Official Weather Watcher's Badge

Name

Weather Watch Center

Set up a Weather Study Center to be used throughout the book to:

- encourage children to study the winter environment.
- encourage students to investigate to better understand the weather around them.
- aid in the answering of questions.
- foster skills of measurement, graphing, reasoning, recognizing relationships and articulating thoughts.

Materials

window
table and chairs
weather diary
weather symbols
    sheet (page 8)
cloud charts
weather books
barometer
thermometer
Weather Watch Calendar (page 12)
binoculars, sunglasses, camera (optional)
glue, markers, scissors, pencil, paper

What to Do

1 Set up a table and chairs by a window that offers a good view of the outdoors.

2 Provide various materials listed above to assist children in directing their own investigations of the weather beyond the window.

3 Encourage "weather watchers" to record their observations and weather reports in their weather diaries.

4 At the close of the school day, review today's weather reports and summarize on the Weather Watch Calendar.

Try This

- Designate an official "weather watcher" each day who must record and report on the day's weather. Provide the Official Weather Watcher's Badge on page 8.
- Decorate the surrounding area with magazine pictures, photographs or drawings of various kinds of weather to stimulate weather observation.
- Provide weather words and symbols to assist children in recording their observations.
- Encourage observations with questions such as "How does the sky look today?" "Which way are the clouds moving?" "Can you see across the school yard today?"
- Add and rotate materials at the center on a regular basis. Add a real barometer, a "tornado maker" (screw attachment between the necks of two one-liter bottles, available at hobby and science shops) and newspaper weather reports.
- Invite a local weather observer as a guest to get children excited about the weather as you launch your center.

Weather Reporting

A weather report is a statement of the weather conditions at a particular place and time. These reports are prepared by weather observers and collected at forecast offices where they form the basis of forecasts made by meteorologists. These reports are printed in newspapers, reported on radio and television, cited on computer networks and recorded on telephone call-in lines.

As part of a language arts program, choose a Weather Forecaster to research and report the immediate and long-range forecasts. Have students to listen to weather forecasts and check newspaper for up-to-the-hour information and encourage humor, technical information, weather maps and humor in their forecasts. Take some video footage.

The Easel Weather Broadcast

Report the weather on an easel!

Materials

window location
easel
weather watch window station (climber, chair, recording table)
weather symbols (page 8) for reference or to be pasted to the easel page
permanent foreground characters (laminated paper dolls or photos of children)
markers
glue (optional)

What to Do

1 Make permanent foreground characters and weather symbols.

2 Set up the easel by the Weather Watch Center.

3 Write the date at the top of a new page each day.

4 Provide various materials listed on the left to assist children in observing the weather.

5 Encourage students to observe and record the weather they see throughout the day.

All-Weather Scavenger Hunt

Try This

On a fair day, separate the class into groups.
Give each group the following list:
Find something that
- needs rain to grow
- could be carried by the wind
- dies in cold weather
- puts oxygen into the atmosphere
- needs sunlight to grow
- changes from a liquid to a solid in cold weather

You Are the Weather Reporter!

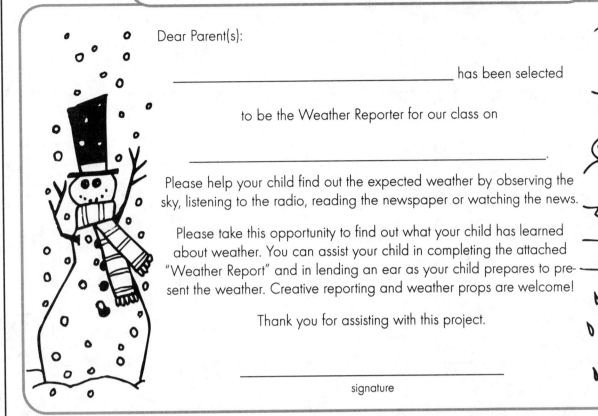

Dear Parent(s):

_____ has been selected

to be the Weather Reporter for our class on

_____.

Please help your child find out the expected weather by observing the sky, listening to the radio, reading the newspaper or watching the news.

Please take this opportunity to find out what your child has learned about weather. You can assist your child in completing the attached "Weather Report" and in lending an ear as your child prepares to present the weather. Creative reporting and weather props are welcome!

Thank you for assisting with this project.

_____

signature

The Weather Report by _____

Today, _____

we can expect no precipitation/precipitation in the form of

_____.

The expected high temperature will reach _____.

and the expected low temperature will be _____.

There will be _____ skies

and no winds/ _____ wind.

The sun rose at _____ and will set at _____.

Enjoy the day!

Sunday	Monday	Tuesday	Wednesday	Thursday	Friday	Saturday

Weather Watch Calendar for the month of _____

Sorting for the Weather

Materials

laminated signs reading: *Hot and Sunny, Wet and Rainy* and *Cold and Snowy*

children's clothing for all kinds of weather:
rubber boots, winter boots, sandals
sun hats, earmuffs, rain hat
winter coat, bathing suit, raincoat
mittens, sunscreen, umbrella
clothes basket
3 hoops

What to Do

1 Set the three hoops about 6" (15 cm) from one another and about 12" (30 cm) from the basket of clothing.

2 Instruct children to put one sign in front of each hoop and to sort the articles into the hoop that represents the particular kind of weather.

3 Allow the child to show you the sorted articles when the task is complete.

Try This

- Older or more advanced students can be given more difficult articles to sort: weather measuring instruments, sports equipment or weather-related hardware (length of eaves trough, lightning rod, container for car antifreeze, furnace filter, snow shovel, garden sprinkler, window screen, etc.).

All Weather Friends

When the rain comes down
We won't frown
We can find our boots
And splash around.

When the sun comes out
We won't pout
We can find our sun hats
And run all about.

When the cold winds blow
We won't be slow
To find our mittens
And play in the snow!

No matter what the weather
We can play together!

R. Eagan

Try This

- This poem can be used for shared reading experience and extended to children's own writing exercises.

- Children can make up their own rhyme about a particular kind of weather. Give each child their own 8" x 10" (20 x 28 cm) (paper to write and illustrate their poem. Put these together in the *All Weather Friends Book* using snap rings. You can add photographs of children playing together in various weather.

- Talk about the term *fair weather friends*. Have they ever acted or had a friend act like a fair weather friend? How did they feel? Why did someone act this way? How can children deal with this kind of behavior?

Chapter 2

The Four Seasons

What Makes the Seasons?

Although we cannot feel it, the Earth is constantly moving. Not only does it spin like a top on its *axis*, making one full turn every 24 hours (an action that creates night and day as the Earth either faces or turns away from the sun), but it also moves along a kind of track or *orbit* around the sun, completing one round trip every year. It is this "around the sun in 365 days" movement that creates the four seasons: winter, spring, summer and autumn (or fall).

The weather changes slightly from day to day or more dramatically from season to season, but it stays much the same from year to year in any one place. This is what is meant by the term *climate*. The climate and the weather are part of a worldwide system of moving masses of warm or cool air. The spinning Earth swirls these circling air masses sideways, making them collide and mix together. It is this changing mixture of air that gives us different weather every day.

But how does the Earth's incredible annual journey account for such dramatic changes in our environment? It has to do with the way the Earth moves around the sun. Because the Earth does not stand straight up and down but leans or tilts on its axis, its closeness to the sun—and thus the amount of sunshine that reaches us—changes over the course of a year.

The world climates range from hot and rainy at the equator to cold and rain free at the poles.

Each of the Earth's *hemispheres,* or halves (north and south, or looking at the globe: top and bottom), tilts away from the sun for part of the year and toward the sun for part of the year. The closeness, or proximity of your part of the Earth to the sun, determines the season. When your part of the Earth is closest to (or tilted towards) the sun, it is summer; when it is furthest from (or tilted away), it is winter. When the Earth is neither tilted toward or away from the sun, it is either spring or autumn.

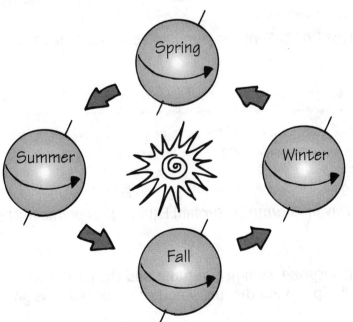

When it is winter in Canada, it is summer in Australia.

Because the sun shines directly at the center of the Earth, or the imaginary line called the "equator," the *tropics* (those areas closest to the equator) are very hot, while the *polar* regions (those at the top and bottom of the Earth) are very cold. Although tropical areas are hot year-round, they might have two different seasons: a rainy season and a dry season. The temperate regions of the world, however, have four seasons—winter, spring, summer and autumn.

Seasons

A division of the year as determined by the Earth's position with respect to the sun, and as marked by temperature, moisture, vegetation, etc.

Winter

December, January and February–Northern Hemisphere; June, July and August–Southern Hemisphere

When it is winter where you live, your part of the Earth is tilted away from the sun. Your part of the Earth gets less sunshine, so the air is colder. In winter, the days are short and the nights are long. If you live in a northern climate, snow falls and covers the ground. Animals sleep in warm dens or nests. People wear layers of clothing to trap heat and keep themselves warm.

(First Day of Winter (Winter Solstice): December 21–NH)

Spring

March, April and May–Northern Hemisphere; September, October and November–Southern Hemisphere

As your part of the Earth begins to tilt toward the sun, the air gets warmer and the days get longer. It rains frequently. The snow melts and tiny green shoots push their way out of the soil. Baby animals are born or hatched. Children shed their snowsuits for raincoats, splash pants and rubber boots. They stomp in puddles and catch tadpoles in swollen drainage ditches.

(First Day of spring (Vernal Equinox): March 21–NH)

Summer

June, July and August–Northern Hemisphere; November, December and January–Southern Hemisphere

When your part of the Earth is fully tilted toward the sun, it is summer. The days are longer and hotter. People wear loose clothing (often as little as possible!), caps and sunscreen to keep themselves cool and safe. The ground gets hard; the grass, long and dry. There is very little rain. On humid days, when the air is full of moisture, thunder rumbles in the distance. The new baby animals grow big, learn to feed themselves and leave their mothers.

(First Day of Summer (Summer Solstice): June 21–NH)

Autumn

September, October and November–Northern Hemisphere; February, March and April–Southern Hemisphere

As autumn, or fall, approaches, your part of the Earth begins to tilt away from the sun. The days grow shorter; the air is cooler. In some parts of the world, the leaves on the trees turn gold and orange and red, then fall to the ground. Children dress in long pants and wear jackets. The rain returns. Animals scurry around gathering food for winter or prepare for long journeys to warmer climates.

(First Day of Autumn (Autumnal Equinox): September 21–NH)

Winter, spring, summer, autumn and the Earth has made one full trip around the sun. Another whole year has gone by!

Be a "Seasonologist"

Changing seasons can affect our moods and feelings: people tend to be happier on warm, sunny days and grumpier on cold, dark days.

What Season Is It?

You can tell what season it is just by the condition of the plants and animals around you, by the weather, and by the kind of clothing people are wearing.

1. Is there snow on the ground? Are the tree branches bare? Has the fur on the animals you can see grown thick and woolly? Are people wearing heavy coats, hats, mittens?

   YES   **NO**

2. If there was snow on the ground, has it melted? Can you see buds on the trees? Are little green bumps visible in the garden? Does the air seem alive with the sound of birds and frogs singing? Are mother animals accompanied by new babies? Are people wearing light jackets or raincoats and rubber boots?

   YES   **NO**

3. Have the blossoms on the trees turned into fruit? Is the grass dry? Has it been a long time since it last rained? Do you hear thunder rumbling in the distance at night? Do you see animals panting, lying in the shade or sleeping in the afternoon? Is the school year over? Are people wearing shorts and T-shirts– swimsuits, maybe?

   YES   **NO**

4. Is it windy outside? Are the leaves changing color and falling off the trees? Are animals busy gathering nuts and berries? Are the birds' nests empty? Are the spring babies almost as large as their parents? Have most of the plants gone to seed? Are the pumpkins ripe and the crops harvested? Is it getting dark earlier? Is there frost on the ground some mornings? Has school started again? Do you need a jacket in the morning and maybe some splash pants?

   YES   **NO**

5. It is: **Winter**   **Spring**   **Summer**   **Autumn**

Make a Season-O-Gram

Draw in and color the appropriate activities and attire to make each of these pictures illustrate a different season (winter, spring, summer, autumn).

Season Scramble (a speed-dressing game for the entire class)

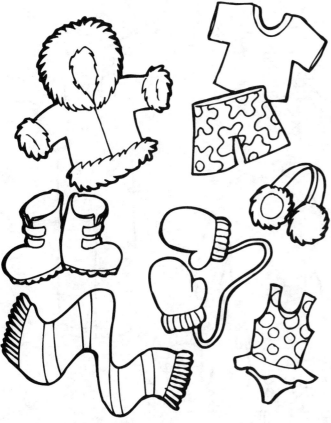

Have children take turns rolling the die. When a number from one to four is rolled, the person rolling the die must jump up, run to the middle of the circle and dress in the three articles of clothing that correspond to the season. See who can dress the quickest. (For younger children, draw a chart on the chalkboard or paper to illustrate which articles of clothing belong to each season:

1. winter: winter boots/winter coat/mittens
2. spring: rubber boots/rain hat/raincoat
3. summer: sandals/summer hat/sunglasses
4. autumn: running shoes/jacket/wool hat

Write the numbers one to four on the chalkboard or a piece of paper taped to the wall. Equate each number with a season (ie. 1 = winter; 2 = spring; 3 = summer; 4 = autumn). Have the children sit in a large circle on the floor.

In the middle of the circle, place the following large-sized items in a pile:

- pair of winter boots
- winter coat
- pair of mittens
- pair of rubber boots
- rain hat
- raincoat
- pair of sandals
- summer hat
- sunglasses
- pair of running shoes
- jacket
- wool hat

Seasonal Cut-Outs

Cut out the figures and the clothing. Color and paste appropriate clothing on the figures.

Paper Puzzle Center (or Seatwork)

Copy (enlarge if desired) and then cut each of these pictures into puzzle pieces according to the age of the children. Then put puzzles in separate bags according to season or jumble together. Have children put puzzles together. As a center activity, the puzzles can be built and taken apart over and over again. As a seatwork activity, the puzzles can be glued down and colored.

Math for Every Season

Basic Problem Solving

1. How many seasons are there in each year? _____

2. How many springs are there in 10 years? _____ How many autumns? _____

3. How many different seasons have you seen in your lifetime? _____

4. How many summers and winters? _____

Make a Season-O-Graph

Find out what season each student in your class likes best. Take these totals and place on the graph.

	Spring	Summer	Fall	Winter

Seasonal Symbol Math

Use the calendars provided (see page 12) to determine how many days it snowed in January, how many days it rained in April, how many July days were sunny and how many October days were windy. (How many were not?)

Advanced Math Questions (not to be copied for younger children):

1. Assuming it rained for half of the remaining days in July, how many days did it rain that month? _____

2. If 4" (10 cm) of rain fell each day, how much rain fell over the course of the month? _____

3. If you had to stay indoors for 2 weeks of July sunshine, how many sunny days could you spend outside? _____

4. If the other summer months enjoyed just as much sunshine, how many days did the sun shine during the summer? _____

5. a. If a snapdragon blossom takes 1 week of sunshine to grow and die, how many blooms would there be over the course of the summer? _____

    b. If the snapdragon plant had 7 blossoms at a time, how many blooms would there have been in July? _____

    c. If there were 3 snapdragon plants in total, and each could have 7 blossoms at one time, how many blooms would there have been over the course of the summer? _____

Spot the Differences

Find at least five differences between each of these picture pairs.

Spot the Differences

Find at least five differences between each of these picture pairs.

Out-of-Season

Circle the things that do not belong.

Four Seasons Find a Word

Find each of the words listed at the bottom and circle in the puzzle.

```
S  C  O  L  D  S  R  Y  Y
U  A  C  O  R  P  R  W  H
S  U  M  M  E  R  T  O  H
L  T  Y  E  T  I  H  N  C
O  U  N  Y  N  N  U  S  U
O  M  I  W  I  G  S  U  M
C  N  A  R  W  I  N  D  Y
W  M  R  A  W  S  N  O  A
```

winter   cold   snowy
spring   warm   rainy
summer   hot   sunny
autumn   cool   windy

Seasonal Mix 'n' Match

Draw a line to connect the season with the activity.

People

winter

spring

summer

fall

Animals

winter

spring

summer

fall

Plants and Trees

winter

spring

summer

fall

Season Scramble

Each of the seasons is associated with different kinds of weather.
Winter: cold weather–snow, sleet, hail, ice, frost
Spring: warm weather–rain, frost, fair/foul weather clouds
Summer: hot weather–thunderstorms, humidity or dryness, sunshine
Autumn: cool weather–wind, frost

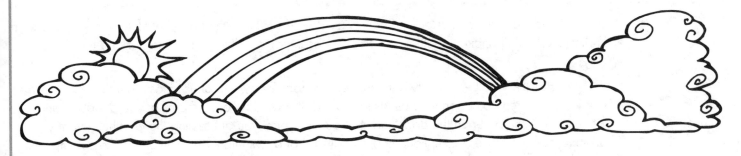

Unscramble the words and draw a line to connect the season with the weather.

aiynr   mtunau   tho

ntweir   mrwa   psignr

nydiw   ynuns   ownsy

mrmesu   lcdo   loco

Chapter 3

Watching and Measuring the Weather

The Weather and You

You see and feel the weather around you every day. The wind, water and heat from the sun create an endless cycle of changing weather that can be observed, felt, detected, measured and recorded.

We measure the weather in many different ways; in fact, every one of us measures it in our own way every day. When you open your blinds to look out the window each morning, you are observing the weather. When you open the door and stick out your arm, you are feeling the weather. From your observations you make assumptions about what kind of day it might be. You can make assumptions based on the sky, the temperature and the time of day. Is it rainy or cloudy? Are the clouds moving quickly? Is the sky blue and clear? Is the sun shining? Simple observations can help you to measure and predict the weather for the entire day, for tomorrow or for an entire week!

 ## Feel the Weather

Experience the weather using all of your senses in nature's classroom!

Materials

the outdoors
weather-appropriate attire
cassette recorder (optional)
blindfolds (optional)

What to Do

1 Take students into an outdoor location in various kinds of weather.

2 Encourage children to observe the weather by looking at it up close and at a distance. Discuss what they see. Did they observe anything they had not seen before? Explain that we often miss important details. Explain that careful observation is the most important part of any scientific study.

3 Encourage children to listen to the weather by closing their eyes or wearing blindfolds. Have they taken the time to listen to the weather before?

4 Encourage children to feel the weather by lying on the ground, or touching with their hands. How does the pavement or grass feel?

5 Ask children to smell the weather. Do they notice any smells? What are they? Which direction is the wind blowing from?

Try This

- Tape-record sounds of the weather and children's responses to the weather on particular days. Compile a "weather wise" recording that could include weather facts, songs and sounds.

Who Needs to Know the Weather?

Almost everyone needs to know the weather because it affects each one of us. For various reasons we might need to know what weather to expect today, tomorrow or at the end of the week. Industries such as agriculture, aviation, construction, fishing and tourism depend greatly upon weather reports to help with their success. These industries can benefit economically from accurate weather reports.

Warning of adverse weather conditions or calls for good weather can be of great importance to many people. From farmers planning the planting or harvesting of crops to children planning sports events or the day's activities, weather reports are most helpful.

Materials

bristol board or recording chart
markers
magazines
scissors
glue

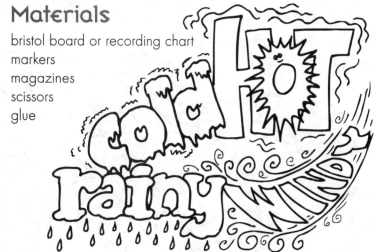

What to Do

1 Divide the board into four equal sections. Mark the sections: *Hot and Sunny, Wet and Rainy, Cold and Snowy* and *Cool and Clear.*

2 Ask children to brainstorm. What do they do in each kind of weather? What sports are they involved in? Do they have chores to do at home? What do they wear?

3 Record their responses to the various weather conditions onto the chart.

4 Provide magazines, newspapers, scissors and glue. Children can find pictures of people doing things in the different kinds of weather to paste onto the appropriate sections.

5 When the paste has dried, children are invited to write *adjective graffiti* in the various sections. Children can fill in any spaces left in the sections with adjectives that describe the weather conditions.

Try This

• Add weather wear to the dramatic play center.

Weather Folklore and Myths and Predictors

From the earliest times people have been awed by the weather. They watched it, respected it and lived according to its moods. These early people tried to understand and predict the weather that ruled their lives by watching nature and turning to the myths, legends and superstitions that tried to explain its unpredictable changes.

Native peoples, sailors, farmers, housewives and others whose livelihood depended on the weather knew that nature gave clues about the coming weather. They understood the complexity of the skies and clouds, the moon and the sun, and animal and plant behavior and knew what clues to watch for.

Myths, legends and weather lore helped people to understand and pass on their understanding of the weather. Many of the old wise sayings are still passed on as reliable predictors of the weather. Some are more accurate than others!

Plant Predictors

Sunflowers open in fine weather and close before a shower.

The scales of a pinecone open in dry weather and close when damp weather is on its way.

Seaweed can be hung outside to predict weather. The seaweed will become limp when rain is approaching and brittle in dry, sunny weather.

The petals of a morning glory open in fine weather and close tightly when damp, rainy or cool weather is about to occur.

Dew Foretell!

Dew always foretells of good weather. It won't form under an overcast sky or in windy weather.

When the dew is on the grass,
Rain will never come to pass.

Animal Weather Predictors

People have always watched the animal kingdom for signs of weather changes. Instinct and specialized organs may be the causes of animal reactions prior to weather change. It is believed animals are able to detect and react to atmospheric changes more quickly than humans.

Woolly Forecast

If a sheep's wool swells and straightens out, moist rainy air is on its way.

Croak for Rain

In early times in France some farmers put treefrogs under glass bells to forecast coming rain. They croaked to announce any coming rain.

The Groundhog

North Americans watch the groundhog on February 2 to find out how much winter is yet to come. If the groundhog emerges from his burrow on this day and the sun is shining, a shadow will be cast to predict six more weeks of winter. If the skies are overcast and no shadow is cast, it is said that spring is just around the corner. Statistics show that the groundhog theory is not reliable but adds some fun to a long winter. This is thought to have developed from the February 2 Candlemas Day of medieval times in European history when this proverb was well known:

If Candlemas Day be fair and bright,
Winter will have another fight;
But if Candlemas Day brings clouds and rain,
Winter is gone and won't come again.

Feathered Forecast

If you hear an owl hoot in the daytime, it will rain within three days.

When chickens roll in the sand,
Rain is close at hand.

Animal "Fur"cast

You can tell how severe a winter is going to be by how thick animals' coats grow in the fall.

Cows and horses huddle in the pasture when rain is on its way.

Fishy Forecast

Fish may be susceptible to atmospheric pressure changes and may offer clues to the coming weather as a result. Many fishermen believe that particular behavior indicates particular weather–but few can agree on which actions predict which type of weather!

Chirp Count

There is a close connection between the air temperature and the tempo of a cricket's chirp. If you count the number of chirps in eight seconds and add four, you will have the temperature to within one degree Celsius, nine times out of 10.

The Ants Go Marching . . .

Ants are very sensitive to temperature changes. The higher the temperature the faster they move; one scientist claims he can tell the temperature to within a degree by timing their movements.

From early times people have watched the sky for clues about the approaching weather. Sky watching is an important part of modern weather predictions.

Evening red and morning gray
That's the sign of a beautiful day,
But evening gray and morning red
Brings down rain upon your head.

Rainbow in the morning, sailors take warning.

A rainbow in the morning
Is the shepherd's warning.
A rainbow at night
Is the shepherd's delight.

A colored ring or rainbow around the moon or the sun is called a halo, corona or ring around the moon or sun. Halos or coronas are reliable forecasters of an approaching storm, and the brighter they are, the nearer the storm. The Zuni tribe of natives had a weather proverb related to these rings:

When the sun is in his house, it will rain soon.

The bigger the ring, the nearer the wet.

Weather Wise Lore

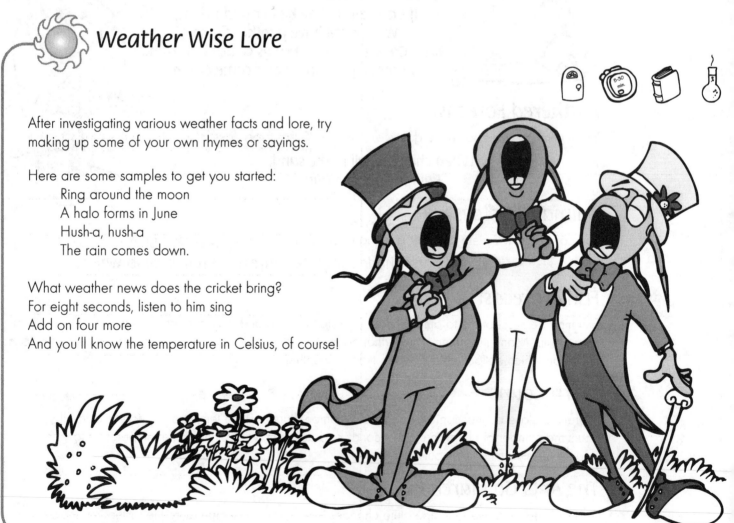

After investigating various weather facts and lore, try making up some of your own rhymes or sayings.

Here are some samples to get you started:
    Ring around the moon
    A halo forms in June
    Hush-a, hush-a
    The rain comes down.

What weather news does the cricket bring?
For eight seconds, listen to him sing
Add on four more
And you'll know the temperature in Celsius, of course!

Name _____

Check the Almanac

Provide copies of the current Farmer's Almanac to your class.

Write questions on the board based on the almanac. Have students find the answers they need the way a farmer might.

Design your own Student's Almanac. Incorporate skills of language arts, communication, research, design, group dynamics and problem solving into this activity.

Student's Almanac

Predicting the Future Weather

A weather forecast is a prediction of coming weather. This prediction is based on current understanding of scientific fact from information about wind speed, wind direction, air pressure, moisture in the air and the nearness of other weather systems.

Weather reports and warnings are broadcast so people can prepare for what is to come. The planting and harvesting of crops; the date of summer picnics, winter travel and other activities are dependent upon weather forecasts. Many lives are saved when people are warned not to travel in winter blizzards or advised to evacuate an area before a hurricane hits.

Quickly changing factors influence the weather, and weather patterns are not always predictable. This makes it difficult to accurately predict the coming weather and it sometimes makes the weather forecaster a little unpopular!

Modern-Day Weather Watching

The scientific study of weather, called meteorology, began in Italy in the 17th century. Instruments were developed to give detailed measurements of changes in the temperature, air pressure and moisture content of the air. But it was not until 1850 that weather instruments became accurate enough to give information that would be useful for predicting the weather. Every day, new equipment is being developed meteorologists provide more accurate forecasts.

Weather Stations

A meteorologist is a weather scientist who studies the condition of the air, atmosphere and weather. They are in charge of weather stations and put weather information together to give an accurate picture of the weather.

Meteorologists at weather stations around the world rely on instruments on the ground and carried in weather balloons, satellites and planes to help them measure wind direction and speed, precipitation, air pressure and many other factors. Weather is measured around the clock at more than 100,000 weather stations around the world. Weather stations record the temperature, rainfall, humidity, air pressure and speed and direction of the wind. Each weather station reports to the nearest central weather office. Thousands of observations and measurements taken at weather stations around the world are fed into computers at weather stations and swapped by means of a special Global Telecommunications System or GTS. The information is combined to provide complex, large-scale weather forecasts that form a picture of how the weather is changing. All of this information helps meteorologists to understand local and global weather and provide immediate and long-range weather forecasts.

*Forecasters study weather data collected at weather stations around the world by meteorologists and make maps or synoptic charts that help to predict the coming weather.

Measuring the Weather

Weather changes can be measured and measurements recorded. Modern-day meteorologists have many fancy instruments to help them track the weather.

The first thermometer was made about 1600 by Galileo Galilei. Forty years later, Galileo's first pupil Torricelli, made a practical barometer for measuring air pressure. This was the beginning of sensitive instruments that give us the scientific weather forecasts of today.

Weather Satellites

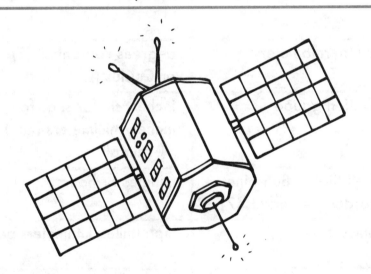

Weather satellites are like giant weather watchers in the sky that orbit the Earth or hang over the same place and gather information that meteorologists use to track weather systems. Satellites gather and beam back information that cannot be obtained from the ground, such as large-scale coverage, wind speeds at sea level and the movements of storms and weather patterns.

Weather Balloons

Weather balloons can carry instruments to measure details about temperature, air pressure, humidity and wind speeds. At midnight and midday Greenwich Time, hundreds of weather balloons are launched around the world. These helium-filled balloons are launched several miles (kilometers) into the upper atmosphere to transmit gathered information to ground by instruments within the balloon called radiosonde. The gathered information is made available on computer to all weather stations.

How Weather Is Measured

Weather Measured	Instrument	Units
air pressure (atmospheric pressure) The weight of air pressing down on the Earth's surface	aneroid barometer	millibars or kilopascals (kPa)
temperature Air temperature	mercury thermometer	degrees Fahrenheit (F) or Celsius (C)
precipitation Rain, snow, hail or sleet that falls	precipitation gauge	inches/cm for snowfall inches/millimeters (mm) for rainfall
sunshine Intensity of sunlight	Campbell Stokes Sunshine Recorder (see page 47)	minutes or hours
wind speed Rate of motion the wind is traveling	anemometer	mph (miles/kilometers per hr.)
wind direction The direction the wind is blowing	wind vane	direction
wind force Observations about the power of the wind based on its effects on everyday objects	Beaufort scale	0-12 numbering system
dew point The temperature on which dew forms on the ground	dew point gauge	degrees C or F
relative humidity Amount of water vapor or dampness the air can hold before it rains. The most it can hold is 100%.	Hygrometer/Pychrometer	percentage

TLC10072 Copyright © Teaching & Learning Company, Carthage, IL 62321-0010

Junior Meteorologists' Weather Watching Station

With careful observation of the skies and simple homemade instruments, we can all be weather watchers. In fact, experienced weather watchers still predict local weather using simple instruments and careful observations of the skies. You can learn to understand the weather and weather forecasts better by observing and interpreting the signs and measurements you encounter.

Record and Analyse

Use a notebook to write information about the skies, winds, precipitation, temperature and air pressure using your senses and the equipment you make throughout this book. Pay careful attention to the weather conditions you track, and you will see some weather patterns.

Taking Measurements

- Take your measurements at the same time at least once every day.
- Humidity, air pressure and temperature changes often occur slowly and take time to register on your instruments. Have patience!

Visual Records

- Take pictures or illustrate the sky to add to your record.

 ## Pet Weather Forecaster Rocks

Materials

1 large rock for each child
glue-on eyes

What to Do

1 Glue eyes on the rocks.

2 Put your weather forecaster rock outside and wait for the forecast.
> If the weather is rainy, the rock is wet.
> If the weather is dry, the rock is dry.
> If the weather is hot, the rock is hot.
> If the weather is cold, the rock is cold.

Weathering

We can measure years and years of weather by its effects on the Earth. Wind, rain, frost, ice and sunshine "weather" the Earth. Wind can whip tiny sand particles against rocks and wear down a surface; rain can collect in a crevice and then expand with freezing and crack the rock; the sun can bake rocks by day and freeze them by night making the outer layers of the rock flake. Weather is continually eroding, cracking, expanding or shrinking natural elements in a way that changes the face of the Earth over millions of years.

Junior Weather Watcher's Barometer: Measure the Air Pressure

The Earth is surrounded by layers of gases that make up the atmosphere or air. This air presses up, down and sideways on everything. The force of the air pressing down is called air pressure. Air is always on the move although we don't really notice it unless there is a strong wind blowing it around. This moving air causes changes in air pressure, which usually mean changes in weather.

We can measure changes in air pressure with a barometer. Rising or falling air pressure helps us to predict the coming weather. Heat moves the molecules in the air making warm air less dense and lighter and reducing the air pressure so the barometer reading will be low. Cool air is heavier and more dense causing increased air pressure so the barometer reading will be high. The cooler the air, the higher the pressure.

As air warms it rises leaving an area of low pressure where cool, heavier air can rush in. Generally, falling air pressure indicates that wet or stormy weather is on the way. Rising pressure usually foretells fine, clear weather.

The barometer was invented by Torricelli in 1644. The unit kilopascal originated with Blaise Pascal (1623 to 1662), a French scientist and philosopher who studied weather. Normal pressure ranges from 98.0 to 103.0 kPa.

Materials

wide-mouth glass jar (2^1/$_2$" to 3" [6 to 8 cm] across)
glue
tape
scissors
marker
14" (36 cm) balloon
8" x 12" (20 x 30 cm) cardboard strip
sturdy drinking straw
a clear day

What to Do

1 Cut the end off of the balloon and stretch it over the jar until you have a flat surface.

2 Cut both ends of the straw at angles.

3 Glue one end of the straw to the center of the balloon.

4 Fold the cardboard strip into thirds to make a triangular column.

5 On a clear day place your jar in a place where the temperature is steady. Stand the column beside the free end of the straw.

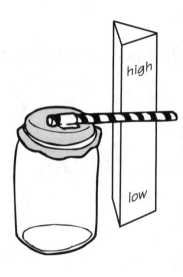

Air that is held in the jar presses against the inside of the jar and the balloon. Air on the outside of the jar presses on the outside of the balloon. When the pressure outside the jar is greater than the pressure inside the jar, then the balloon is depressed or pushed down causing the straw to rise upward to indicate a rise in air pressure. When air pressure outside the jar is less than the air pressure inside the jar, the balloon will rise slightly tilting the straw down to indicate a fall in air pressure.

6 Mark the column where the straw is pointing and record the weather with a simple symbol. Mark it again whenever the straw changes positions. Different weather appears with changes in air pressure, so watch your barometer to see which kinds of weather go with high and low pressures. Look for patterns that might help you predict coming weather.

40

Mapping the Weather

Weather forecasters draw special maps, or synoptic charts, to help predict what kind of weather is on its way. You can find these on television or in newspaper weather reports. Weather maps show areas of high and low pressures, the locations of cold and warm fronts, cloud cover, wind, precipitation and temperature across a country. In temperate latitudes like North America, weather tends to travel from west to east. If you want to know what kind of weather to expect, look at the weather west of your location.

The Language of Weather Maps

air mass: a large body of air with the same temperature and moisture content
front: edges of a warm or cold air masses, the line of changing weather between two kinds of air masses
isobar: a line, drawn on a weather chart, that joins points of the same air pressure
H: high pressure area (usually means good weather)
L: low pressure area, generally means bad weather

Most weather maps are easy to read because they rely on symbols to represent various kinds of weather. Common symbols include rain, cloud cover, wind, sunshine, temperature and air pressure. Here are some of the international weather symbols. Look in your local newspaper for these:

Drizzle	Thunderstorm
Rain	Hail
Snow	Haze
Showers	Fog

Make Your Own Weather Map

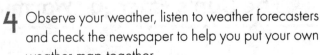

What to Do

1 Study weather maps in local newspapers. Using the information in this book, you can learn to understand what they mean.

2 Make your own weather map beginning with an enlarged photocopied map of your area.

3 Create some weather symbols using the international weather symbols above, the weather symbols on page 8 or by making up your own.

4 Observe your weather, listen to weather forecasters and check the newspaper to help you put your own weather map together.

Try This

• Use permanent marker to draw a simple map of your area onto Plexiglas™. Have the "weather reporter" draw the symbols on the map and explain the weather just as the weather forecaster would on television.

Chapter 4

Sunny Days

Sunny Weather

Sunny weather! Most of us love to shed our coats, run barefoot, swim, play sports and enjoy the sunshine. Every place in the world experiences sunny weather and clear skies. Some places get very little sunny weather and some get lots, especially in the summer. Sunny weather usually hangs around for a while because the high atmospheric pressure with its calm, dry, sinking air keeps away other kinds of weather.

What Is the Sun?

The sun is an ordinary, middle-sized yellow star–one of 100 billion stars in our galaxy, the Milky Way. It is at the center of our solar system, and its gravity keeps all of the planets in their orbits. It seems larger and brighter than all of the other stars because it is the closest star to Earth–about 93 million miles away!

The sun's energy keeps every living thing on Earth alive. Its gravity keeps the planets in their orbits. It causes day and night and the seasons. Its energy keeps the atmosphere in constant motion which causes the weather and the climates. It causes water to evaporate, rain to fall, storms to blow and rainbows to form. It enables plants to grow which allows animals and humans to survive. Without the sun there would be no heat, no light, no clouds and no rain. Without the sun there would be no life on Earth.

The sun is a giant in our universe.
We would need 1,300,000 Earths to make a ball as large as the sun.

The Sun's Energy: Warming the Earth

Our sun is a massive boiling, bubbling, sphere of exploding gases believed to be 72°F (40 million°C) at the core!

Inside the sun, hydrogen is changed into helium gas causing explosions that radiate light, heat, X rays and other kinds of radiation throughout space. Some of this radiated energy reaches the Earth and becomes heat in a journey that takes about eight minutes. The atmosphere controls the Earth's temperature by absorbing almost half of the sun's energy, or reflecting it back into space.

Solar rays that travel through the atmosphere warm the surface of the land and sea, helping to warm the air around us. Some heat bounces off the Earth and escapes back into space but most is trapped in our atmosphere by water vapor and carbon dioxide gases in what is known as the *greenhouse effect*.

Sock It to the Sun

Wear one white sock and one black sock and sit outside in the sun for story time.
Which sock gets hotter?
White reflects or bounces away sunlight; black absorbs it.

Feel the Heat

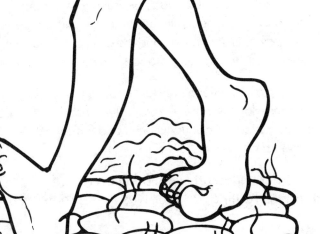

What to Do

When the sun is at its hottest (about noon), take a walk to find places where the sun's heat has radiated.

Try This

- Try walking on a sandy beach or lying on a hot rock at noon or after a sun shower.

We feel the warmth of the sun when it shines on us. Sunshine also warms surfaces that are directly exposed to it, and they feel warm when touched. In some places, sand, pavement or rocks may be too hot to walk on barefoot during the hottest hours of the day. When the sun's energy strikes an object, we feel heat.

Materials

hot, sunny day
pavement, sand or rock surface

Plants Need Sunshine!

Sunshine provides the energy plants need to grow. The leaves of green plants consist of cells that contain chlorophyll. Through a process called photosynthesis, chlorophyll converts sunlight into the chemical energy plants need for growth.

There is an old saying that the sun never hides more than three days.
Is this true? How can you find out?

Legends of the Sun

Many people around the world have worshipped the sun as the sustainer of life. They understood that all life depended on the sun. Reliable sunshine was needed for warmth, daylight and to bring crops to harvest.

The European Celts, South American Mayans, North American natives and other ancient people watched the sun very closely. Stone and earth structures, like Stonehenge in England, were built to keep track of the passing of the year. In Saskatchewan, Canada, two such rock arrangements, dating from the first century A.D., were discovered to be aligned with the sun at the summer solstice. The Aztecs of Mexico worshipped the god of dawn, Quetzalcoatl and the sun god Tonatuich. Great temples were constructed and sacrifices made to persuade the sun god to shine brightly on them.

In an ancient legend, Orion the hunter was placed among the stars and his faithful dog Sirius followed. Sirius became leader of the Great Dog constellation and at the start of the hottest period of the year, Sirius rose just before dawn. This hot period lasted for about 40 days and in North America, became known as the Dog Days of Summer lasting from July 3 to August 11.

People whose lives depended on the sea believed that
if the sun shone when it was raining, a sailor was going to heaven.

 ## The Sun and the Wind

Memorize this little tale and then tell it with lots of expression and hand gestures.

Early one morning as the stars faded, the sun and the wind awoke at the same time. The wind blew, "I am far more powerful than you, old sun, go back to sleep."

But the sun beamed and said nothing. Just then a young girl stepped out of her home to play. She was wearing a warm sweater to ward off the morning chill.

The wind saw the sweater and had an idea. "Sun, I can prove that I am more powerful than you. I will get that sweater off of the child." The silent sun beamed as the wind blew, lightly at first and then a little stronger. As the wind picked up, the leaves rustled and the flowers bent and the little girl pulled her sweater more tightly around herself. The wind blew harder, and she buttoned her sweater. The wind became angry and blew and blew so hard that the little girl's hair flew out behind her, and she had to hold on to the apple tree in her garden to keep from blowing away. The wind blew and blew some more until it could blow no more.

The sun continued to beam, this time a little stronger. The girl let go of the tree and straightened her hair. The sun beamed on and the girl undid her sweater buttons. The sun shone down some more, and the girl wiped some sweat from her forehead just before she removed her sweater.

The Colors of Sunlight

Although it seems that sunlight has no color, it actually contains all seven colors you see in a rainbow combined to look white. Sunlight travels in straight lines and can be seen when it hits a reflective surface. Although our air is transparent, it is full of gas molecules, dust, ice crystals and water droplets that affect the solar rays. When sunlight passes through these particles, it is scattered into all of its wavelengths, in various directions. The constant stirring of the atmosphere causes an endless array of colors in our sky.

The gases in the air scatter mostly the blue component of light towards our eyes and not the green, yellow and red colors. The bouncing around of the blue light makes the whole sky appear blue.

When the sun rises and sets, the sunlight passes through the dense lower layer of the atmosphere containing more particles to scatter the red light but not the blue, causing brilliant sunrises and sunsets. Sometimes sunlight strikes ice or water particles that bend the light to produce spectacular effects like the rainbow, mock sun or sundog.

 ## Dancing Sunbeams

Open your discussion of sunlight with a colorful dance! Borrow and collect as many crystals or "suncatchers" as you possibly can and hang them from your classroom on a sunny day for a spectacular display.

Try This

- A room full of dancing sunbeams is a very inspiring atmosphere. Use this experience as a leadoff for a creative writing activity or art activity.

- Look at all the colors. When sunlight enters a raindrop or spray from a hose, the light rays get bent and the colors split apart so that you can see each one.

45

The Magic of Evaporation

The sun's heat will cause water to vanish before your eyes! It doesn't actually vanish, it evaporates or changes form. The sun's heat causes particles at the water's surface to vibrate fast enough to escape into the air in the form of a gas called a vapor.

Relief from the Heat

When we are hot we sweat. Our sweat evaporates to cool us down. When the relative humidity is high on a hot summer day, we feel sticky because the air is already holding nearly all of the water that it can hold, and the sweat on our skin can't evaporate.

Puddle Tracings

Watch evaporation in action!

Materials

puddle of water on a paved surface on a sunny day
chalk or tempera paint

What to Do

1 Find or make a puddle of water on a paved surface on a sunny day.

2 Trace the puddle with chalk or tempera paint.

3 Watch what happens as the sun's heat beats down on the puddle.

The Art of Evaporation

Watercolor artist's use evaporation to create special effects in their paintings.

Materials

muffin tins
1/8 cup (30 ml) warm water in each tin
3 tsp. (15 ml) salt for each tin
dry tempera paint or food coloring
heavy white paper (tagboard, construction paper or
   watercolor painting paper)
paintbrushes

What to Do

1 Stir the water, salt and coloring to a desired shade in the separate muffin tins.

2 Paint a picture using the salt paints.

3 Watch what happens as the water evaporates from the paints and the salt remains.

Tracking the Sun

Does the sun stay in one place all day long?
Track the sun and find out!

Materials

window with a
    view of the sun
sunny day
8 paper suns
masking tape

What to Do

1 Cut out eight paper suns.

2 Mark an *X* on the floor; stand on it and look at the sun through your window.

3 Record the time of day on a paper sun and stick it to a window where you see the sun.

4 Repeat this process at one-hour intervals throughout the day. Leave the previous sun on the window and you will have a record of the sun's movements at the end of the day.

Try This

- Discuss the movements of the sun as outlined in Chapter 2, page 15.

Sunshine Recorder

Meteorologists measure the hours of sunshine each day with a Campbell Stokes Sunshine Recorder or parheliometer.

The Sunshine Recorder is a glass ball that focuses the sun's rays onto a cardboard strip marked with a time scale. As the sun moves across the sky, it burns a record of its path onto the strip. This burnt path record reveals the hours of sunshine for the entire day.

 ## Sun Prints

Materials

colored construction paper or recycled fax paper
interesting shaped small objects (keys, leaves, small
    toys, rings, jewelry, seeds, flowers, shells, grasses,
    feathers, pebbles, paper cut-outs, etc.)
piece of Plexiglas™ a little larger than the photo-
    graphic paper (if necessary)
piece of heavy cardboard slightly larger than the glass

What to Do

1 Place the paper on the cardboard.

2 Arrange the items you are printing in an interesting pattern on your piece of paper. Ie. if you want a print of a leaf, lay it on the paper.

3 Cover the paper with the arranged objects with the piece of clear Plexiglas™ to hold objects in place if necessary.

4 Place the paper directly in the sun for an entire day.

5 The sun will fade all areas of the paper except for those covered by the objects.

6 Glue your sun print to a cardboard frame. Attach a string to the back for hanging.

The Sun Booklet

Think about the importance of the sun as you complete your booklet *The Sun*. Provide drawings to illustrate the facts. Cut out the pages and staple together to compile a sun-fact booklet.

The Sun

by _____

The sun is a star.
It is the center of our solar system.

1

It is a huge ball of bubbling, swirling gases.

2

Without the sun there would be no life on Earth.

3

Energy from the sun makes our weather.
It makes water evaporate and it makes it rain.
It causes thunderstorms and rainbows.

4

Plants need the sun's energy to grow.
Animals and people need the plants for
food and oxygen.

5

The sun keeps the planets in their places.

6

All life on Earth depends on the sun.

7

Solar Power: Energy from the Sun

Nearly all of our energy comes from the sun, it is the source of all Earth's natural energy. The sun naturally provides warmth for our planet and energy for our plants. In recent times scientists have studied methods of harnessing direct solar radiation as an energy source for specific uses.

Solar cells tap into this energy source and convert sunshine into electricity using light-sensitive crystals. Today this solar energy is being used for everything from heating swimming pools and homes to powering watches, calculators and vehicles. At this time, solar power is practical only in places where sunshine records are consistent.

Even the fuels we use such as coal, oil and gas are the remains of once-living things.

 ## Catch the Heat

Materials

mirror
magnifying glass
cotton thread
window or outdoors
sunny, clear day

What to Do

1 Cut a length of cotton thread.

2 Tie one end of the thread to the center of the stick, the other end to the weight.

3 Place the stick across the jar so the weight hangs in the middle of the jar.

4 Hold the magnifying glass to focus the sun's heat on the thread.

5 Observe the sun's energy at work.

 ## Solar Power

Watch the energy of the sun at work.

Materials

2 clear containers
thermometer
water
sunny day and a shady place

What to Do

1 Place one container of water in direct sunlight and one in the shade for one hour.

2 Take the temperature of the water in each of the containers.

3 Compare these temperatures and discuss the differences.

The Sun Is Essential to Life on Earth

All energy comes from the sun and all living things depend on this energy to live. Make a mural of all things that depend on the sun for life.

Materials

large roll of mural paper
large compass
colorful markers, paints, pencils, crayons or collage materials
tape
yellow yarn
scissors
yellow, orange and red art materials
glue

What to Do

1 Invite students to brainstorm about all of the things that depend on the sun for life.

2 Place mural paper on the floor and position all children on the same side of the paper to keep drawings and collages upright!

3 Use the compass to mark one large circle (2 meters in diameter). Cut this circle out.

4 Turn the circle into a brightly colored sun using markers; crayons; colored pencils and orange, yellow and red collage materials.

5 Tape enough strands of yellow yarn to the back of the sun for each child.

6 Hang the completed mural to a long hallway and affix the sun above it.

7 Each child will tape one "ray of sun" to their picture.

Try This

- As you work on the mural and the sun, instigate discussions about the sun. "This pasta shape looks like the swirling gases on the sun's surface," "That makes the sun look very hot!" "Are there any living things that do not depend on the sun?" . . . and so on.

Ultraviolet Rays

The sun is essential to life on Earth, but it is so powerful that it can be dangerous. Sunlight consists of different wavelengths of radiation, including ultraviolet A, B and C rays. Ultraviolet rays have more energy than rays of heat or light and can be harmful to living things.

The ozone layer in our upper atmosphere acts like a giant sunscreen that shields living things from most of these harmful rays. Unfortunately, the Earth's protective ozone layer is depleting due to environmental pollution, and we are exposed to more and more damaging rays. We need to protect our skin from these ultraviolet rays all year.

In May 1992, Environment Canada began to include UV information with the daily weather forecast. The UV Index indicates the intensity of UV radiation on a scale of 1-10 where 10 represents the typical midday value in the summertime in the tropics. The higher the UV index, the greater the risk to exposed skin.

UV Index

UV Index	Category
over 9	Extreme
7-9	High
4-7	Moderate
0-4	Low

Source: Environment Canada

Protect Your Skin

Your skin is your body's largest organ and it needs to be protected. You can handle a little ultraviolet energy but too much can be harmful to your skin. Skin cells that are disturbed by the sun's ultraviolet rays can become cancerous.

Animals cover themselves with mud, hide deep in the shade or hide in a cave during the day to protect themselves from the sun. Too much sun stimulates the human body to produce a tanning pigment called melanin which rises to the surface of our skin and helps to protect us from the harmful rays. We can help our body to protect itself all year.

Discussion and Activity

- Discuss harmful effects of the sun. Talk about sunburns and how they feel and what happens to your skin.
- Invite a Cancer Society volunteer or local doctor to speak about the danger of excessive exposure to the sun.
- Make a collage of magazine pictures showing people who should be or are wearing sunscreen, hats or other protection.
- Provide sun wear for your dramatic play center.

INCOMPLETE

Dear Parents:

We are learning to be "sun sensible" and protect ourselves from exposure to the sun that can damage our skin. Prolonged and unprotected exposure to the sun's ultraviolet rays during childhood is known to carry a significant risk of skin cancer later in life.

We will launch our Sun Sensible unit with Crazy Cover Up Day. We will learn that wide-brimmed hats; loose, tightly woven clothing; sunscreen with an SPF of 15 or more; UV ray protective sunglasses and limited midday exposure can protect us from the sun's harmful rays.

If possible, please send a sun hat, sunscreen, sunglasses and appropriate clothing to protect your child from the sun. We will be using these items for dramatic play, math activities, language activities and, of course, to protect us from the sun.

Have a safe, sunny season!

Thank you,

53

Be Sun Sensible: Put Up a Barrier!

Put a barrier between you and the sun.

Cover Up

Protect your skin with clothing, simply slip on a shirt. It is best to wear baggy, long-legged, long-sleeved clothing made from tightly woven cotton. Hold your clothes up to a flashlight. If you can see right through them, then the sun can, too! Its rays can go right through. Which materials would provide you with the best protection from the sun?

Make a Sunshade

Sun umbrellas can be made from large leaves, paper or cloth.

Screen the Sun

Use sunscreen. These creams will give you a protective barrier from the sun. Research estimates that regular use of a highly protective sunscreen for the first 18 years of life can reduce the risk of certain types of skin cancer.

Sunscreen should be applied frequently to all skin that will be exposed to the sun. It takes about 30 minutes to be completely absorbed, so put it on before you go out. The Sun Protection Factor (SPF) tells you how long you should be able to stay in the sun without burning after using the sunscreen. Most skin specialists recommend you use a sunscreen with an SPF of 15 or higher. Check the label or ask the pharmacist for a broad spectrum sunscreen that will protect against harmful UVA and UVB rays. The face, ears, neck, upper chest and arms are sun-sensitive areas. Sensitive skin can be covered with a total sun block, like zinc oxide.

Get Some Cool Shades

Never look directly at the sun with your eyes or through a camera or binoculars. The sun can be very damaging to your eyes. Look for glasses that provide UV ray protection.

Kid Lids

Wear a hat to protect yourself from sun stroke and to protect the skin on your face from the sun's harmful rays. A wide-brimmed hat shades the face, neck, ears and tip of the nose.

Make a Kid Lid

Make your own sun hats using cloth, boxes, paper plates, old hats and so on. Nose shields, leaves, ear shields and neck protectors can be incorporated.

54

Sunscreen for Kids

Design your own bottle of sunscreen for kids. Can you make kids want to wear your brand of sunscreen?

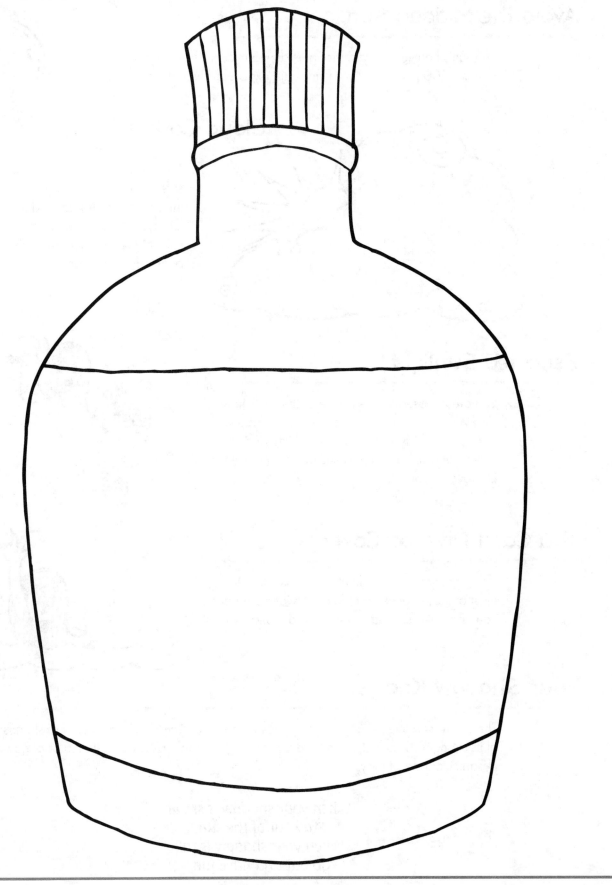

Monitor the Sun's Rays

Avoid the Midday Sun

The sun's harmful rays are strongest during midday, from about 11:00 a.m. to 3:00 p.m. You should limit your exposure during these times.

Cloud Cover

The sun is hiding behind the clouds so you are safe from its harmful rays, right? NO, that is not true. A light cloud cover does not block ultraviolet rays. UV rays are more powerful in the sunlight, but researchers show that 30% of UV rays penetrate clouds and fog.

Reflected Sunlight

You are exposed to even more of the sun's harmful rays when those rays are reflected back at you. Surfaces such as water, sand, concrete and snow reflect sunlight back at you, increasing the intensity of UV rays on your skin.

You Can't Dive for Cover

Although water does reflect some ultraviolet rays, most of these penetrate below the water's surface. You can get a sunburn even if you are underwater!

Your Shadow Knows

The sun is most intense at particular times of the day. A child's shadow is at its shortest when the sun is at its strongest. Teach children to recognize their shadow as a good indicator of how safe the sun is at a particular time of play.

When your shadow is small
Stay out of the sun.
When your shadow is tall
Go out and have fun.

56

Sun Sense

Help protect Sandy and Sam from the sun! They are going to the beach and need your help. Dress them for sun safety. Add items to the picture that will help protect them from the sun.

Sandy and Sam should try to stay out of the sun between _____ and _____ o'clock.

How Hot Is It?

Brainstorm about how hot it is. How does it feel outside? How do you feel? What happens when you run around? Do you hear anything? How does the sky look?

A thermometer is an instrument used to measure temperature. Temperature is a measure of how hot or cold something is. It is usually measured in degrees Fahrenheit (°F) or degrees Celsius (°C).

The Celsius, or centigrade scale, is used by the World Meteorological Organization and most countries in the world. On this scale, 0° is the freezing point; 100° is the boiling point. The Fahrenheit scale is used in the U.S. On this scale, 32° is the freezing point of water; 212° is the boiling point.

Put one thermometer outdoors and one indoors in locations where both are visible. What is the temperature like? Is it hotter inside or outside?

When the temperature increases, the mercury expands and rises up the thermometer tube. When the temperature decreases, the mercury contracts and falls in the thermometer.

Hot Bugs

Can you hear the heat? Cicadas, or heat bugs, make a loud noise by rubbing together two plates on their abdomens. In the months of July and August, these insects celebrate the heat when the temperature rises above 80°F (25°C).

And now for the Cricket Report
Cricket chirps C, # of chirps in 15 seconds divided by 2 + 6 = the temperature
# of chirps in 15 seconds, add 40 = temperature in F
How hot is it? Look at a thermometer. Is it hotter indoors or out? In the sun or shade?

And the Temperature Is . . .

Direct sunlight will warm your thermometer and give an inaccurate reading. To find the true temperature, you will have to screen your thermometer.

Materials

round, white plastic container
2 thermometers
string
hanging location

What to Do

1 Cut the bottom off of the container.

2 Attach string to the top of the container to help you hang it.

3 Attach a second string to hang inside the container. Attach your thermometer from this string so that it hangs in the center of the "sunscreen."

4 Place a second thermometer in the direct sunlight.

5 Take readings from both thermometers and compare them using a chart or graph.

At weather stations, thermometers and other instruments are kept inside a white slatted casing with a double roof that allows for air flow and gives protection from direct sunlight.

Beat the Heat

Your body heat stays just about the same no matter what the weather, because humans are warm-blooded mammals. Your body likes it best when the temperature is about 77°F or 25°C. Whenever the temperature varies from these temperatures, your body will adjust, but intense heat or biting cold can be hard on any body.

The temperature of cold-blooded creatures like insects, frogs and lizards rises and falls with the air temperature. They depend on the sun for their body heat and must bask in the sun to warm their bodies to keep active. When the temperature dips too low, the muscles of these cold creatures won't warm up enough for them to be able to move.

Measure the temperature of your body using a forehead thermometer strip. (These can be purchased in pharmacies.) What affects body temperature?

Highest recorded temperature in the shade: 136°F (58°C) Azizia, Tripolitania, in Northern Africa on September 13, 1922.

The hottest place in the world is Dallol in Ethiopia (East Africa) where the annual temperature average is 94°F (34.4°C).

When the thermometer rises and you're sweaty and hot, you need some tricks to help you beat the heat!

- Reach for the H_2O! You lose water when you sweat and that water needs to be replaced. Cool, clear water is just the thing!
- Sweating helps us to cool down. The sweat on your skin evaporates causing a cooling effect. A patch of skin about the size of a quarter has about 300 sweat glands to do the job.
- Take it easy! Strenuous exercise will produce more heat in your body and can lead to heat exhaustion.
- Protect yourself with barriers from the sun. Cover up with clothes, caps and sunscreen.

 Sun Brew

Materials

hot, sunny day
large jar with a lid
spoon
measuring cup
solar heating mat (black mat of cloth or cardboard)
tea bags (lemon, blackberry, orange or peppermint)
sugar, honey, orange or lemon (optional)

What to Do

1 Fill the jar with water (approximately 1 cup [240 ml] per tea bag).

2 Add the tea bags.

3 Place the sealed jar on the "solar heating mat" in the hot sun.

4 Let the tea steep for about three hours.

5 Serve the tea with orange, lemon, honey or sugar if desired!

Try This

• Experiment with different teas. Adjust the recipe to your own tastes.

• Make use of measuring and recording skills to compose a *Sun Tea Recipe Book*.

• Use a tea ball of freshly picked leaves. Mint leaves make a good tea for hot days as they have a cooling effect on the body.

 Fruit Juice Freezie

Make this messy, mushy, sticky, slurpy, perfect-for-hot-days treat.

Materials

spoon
coffee can
1 cup (240 ml) of juice of your choice

What to Do

1 Fill the can with your favorite juice.

2 Put the spoon in the can.

3 Place the can in the freezer until the juice is almost frozen (about 1 1/2 hours).

4 Remove the can from the freezer, stir the frozen mixture briskly with the spoon. Put it back in the freezer for about 30 more minutes.

5 Remove the can and dig in for cool refreshment!

Try This

• Make up your own juice mixtures. Try strawberry-apple, orange-lemonade or cranberry-lemonade.

• Frozen Fruit: Freeze pieces of just about any fruit from banana slices to raspberries and surprise your mouth!

60

Where There Is Sun, There Is Shadow

 ## Sun Versus Shade

Materials

shady spot and a sunny spot
2 bowls
4 ice cubes of the same size
stopwatch
2 thermometers

What to Do

1 Put two ice cubes in each bowl.

2 Put one bowl in the shade and one in sun at the same time.

3 Start the stopwatch and observe the bowls every few minutes.

4 How long does it take for the ice cubes to melt in the sun? In the shade?

5 Place one thermometer in the sunlight and the other in the shade.

6 Take hourly readings of each thermometer and graph the readings.

7 Discuss the differences in melting times and temperatures for the sun and the shade.

 ## Shadow Art

Materials

sunny day
paved surface
chalk

What to Do

1 Go outside first thing in the morning and have each child choose a partner.

2 Have each child mark an *X* on the pavement several feet away from any other *X*s.

3 Each child will stand on their own *X* and have their partner trace their shadow.

4 Take children outside again at noon and then as late as possible in the daylight to trace their shadow again.

5 Note and discuss the differences in the shadows.

Sundial

Long before we had digital clocks and wristwatches, people used shadows on a sundial to help tell time. They couldn't wear it on their wrist, but they didn't need to worry about batteries or winding!

The shadow cast by the sundial's needle shifts as the sun moves through the sky from sunrise to sunset. The shadow of this needle indicates the time of day.

Try This

- Borrow a garden version of the sundial to share with your children.
- Plant some trees to provide shade in the school yard.

TLC10072 Copyright © Teaching & Learning Company, Carthage, IL 62321-0010

Chapter 5
Cloudy Weather

Clouds are one of the keys we can use to unlock the mysteries of weather. Knowing about clouds–their color, shape, size, height and changing patterns–helps us to predict changes in weather. Cloud formations allow meteorologists to track the movement of weather systems, and from the beginning of time, clouds have been standard fare in the weather watcher's tool kit.

Clouds can form in any climate, anywhere on Earth and can take an endless variety of shapes. The type of cloud that forms depends on a number of factors and conditions. Recognizing different kinds of clouds helps us understand the weather and make predictions about what kind of weather is headed our way.

From Gas to Liquid (or Solid)

Warm air has the ability to hold water vapor but only to a point. At 100% relative humidity, the air cannot hold any more water vapor and is said to be "saturated." At this point, or when temperatures cool the air sufficiently, the water vapor begins to condense into water droplets (or ice crystals) and changes from a gas to a liquid (or a solid). At ground level, mist or fog forms. High in the sky, clouds appear.

A Water Droplet Convention (otherwise known as a cloud)
Clouds are like a massive congregation of tiny water droplets or ice crystals.

Count the number of water droplets in this cloud. If you multiply your answer by one million, you will see how many water droplets you might find in a real cloud. (ie. 12 x 1,000,000 = 12,000,000. It takes *millions* of water droplets to form a small cloud.)

 ## Cloud Math

Match the raindrops with the cloud.

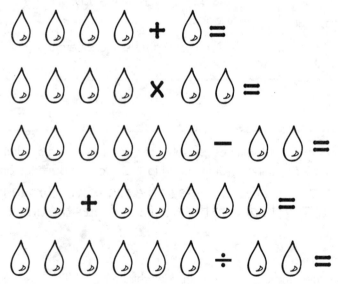

Cloud in a Bottle

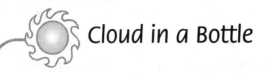

Make your own cloud.

Materials

hot water
glass jar
fistful of ice
elastic band
old pair of panty hose

What to Do

1 Fill a jar with hot water.

2 Carefully (so as not to burn yourself on the hot jar) stretch the panty hose over the neck of the jar and secure with the elastic band.

3 Leave the hot water in the jar for a moment; then pour most of the water away.

4 Put the ice on top of the panty hose. A cloud will form as the warm air rises and meets with the falling cold air. As the hot water evaporates and rises, it is cooled by the ice. It condenses and a cloud forms.

Try This

- Fill a narrow-necked bottle (soda bottles work well) with about 3" (8 cm) of very hot water. Place an ice cube on top of the bottle.

- Place ice in a metal dish and let the dish stand until it is really cold. Put about 1" (2.5 cm) of warm water in a glass jar. Place the metal dish over the top of the jar.

- Hold an aluminum pie plate over a cup of piping hot water. Blow through a straw into the water to create an updraft of warm, moist air.

What Are Clouds?

Clouds are the result of the condensation or freezing of water vapor. The kind of cloud that forms depends on the height of the vapor and the amount of upward air movement present. British amateur meteorologist Luke Howard developed a method for describing and classifying clouds in 1803. His method, which was adopted as the foundation for an international system of cloud identification that is still used today, is based on the general shape of a cloud, its appearance, its thickness and the height at which it forms. In the International Cloud Atlas, as the system was named in 1986, clouds are grouped according to genera and species, and are categorized in the same way as plants and animals.

The little white puffs of air you breathe out in cold weather are miniature clouds.

Cloud Families

Luke Howard identified four main cloud types and gave them each Latin names. Wispy clouds that look like locks of hair are called *cirrus*, the Latin word for *hair*. Heaped, lumpy-looking clouds are called *cumulus*, meaning "pile." Featureless sheets of cloud are called *stratus*, from *stratum*, the Latin word for *layer*. And low, gray rain clouds are called *nimbus*, meaning simply "rain cloud." Today, clouds are divided into 10 genera. Each of these genera are further divided into a variety of species.

Bottoms Up!

Clouds are first arranged according to the height of their bottoms, or bases. There are three different classification heights: low, middle and high. The bases of "high" family clouds can start at heights of anywhere from 16,000 to 35,000 feet (5 to 12 km); "middle" family bases range between 7,000 to 16,000 feet (2 to 5 km); and "low" family bases lie below 7,000 feet (2 km). Clouds of "vertical development"–those that are shaped like rising mounds, domes or towers and often look like cauliflower heads–have their bases in both middle and low family ranges.

Similar-looking clouds have different names depending on the height of their bases.

Airplanes often fly above the clouds.
The sky is always clear there, even if it is raining down below.

Flying High (or Low or Inbetween)

Clouds that form at very high altitudes have names beginning with *cirr-* or *cirro-*. Medium-level clouds begin with *alto-* (from *altus* meaning "high"). And low-lying clouds start with *cumu-* if they are heaped and *strat-* if they form sheets.

A ceilometer measures the height of a cloud.

Cumuliform Clouds

When the ground is hot, pockets or bubbles of warm, vapor-laden air rise rapidly. The vapor condenses at a certain height, but the droplets continue to be carried upward. The result is a heap-shaped cloud.

Stratiform Clouds

When air is lifted slowly and evenly over a large area, which is a typical movement in a low-pressure system, water vapor condenses at a certain height and remains there, creating a layered cloud formation.

Cirriform Clouds

At very high altitudes, water vapor changes into tiny ice crystals that form thin, wispy clouds miles above the ground.

Help Me Find My Family

The three little clouds on the left have lost their families. Match the lost clouds with their families and then match the cloud names with the right families.

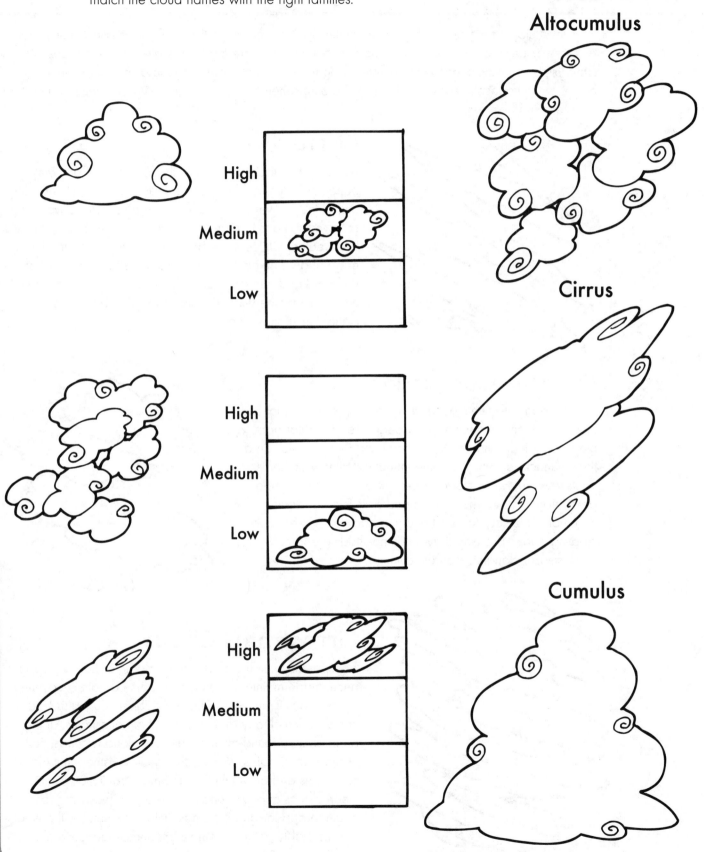

Altocumulus

Cirrus

Cumulus

High

Medium

Low

High

Medium

Low

High

Medium

Low

"Genera"lly Speaking . . .

High Clouds

High-level clouds form at very high levels in the atmosphere where the air contains little water vapor. As a result, they are very thin, wispy and transparent. They are made as water vapor changes into tiny ice crystals. These clouds form at different heights in different regions because of changes in the height of the troposphere (the first layer of the atmosphere), differences in latitude, air temperature and the prevailing air mass.

Cirrus Clouds

Appear as detached clouds in the form of delicate white bands or patches. These are definite indicators of very dry air. (If the air were moist, different kinds of clouds would form at lower altitudes.) In an otherwise clear sky, *cirrus* can mean fine weather will continue but can also appear at the leading edge of a warm front. If cirrus increases to cover most of the sky, wind and rain may soon follow. Made of ice crystals drawn out by the wind into filaments. The longer the filaments, the stronger the wind.

Cirrocumulus Clouds

Thin, transparent-white cloud patch made up of individual cloudlets. Can often have the appearance of regular dappled or rippled pattern. When they look like the scales on a fish, a "mackerel" sky, it can mean that unsettled weather is on its way. They are made of ice crystals that are warmed gently from below. The air rises and sinks into the cloud. Some of the ice crystals melt and turn back into water vapor, creating gaps. This cloud layer has no shading and has much smaller cloudlets than altocumulus.

Cirrostratus Clouds

Transparent, whitish clouds with a smooth or hair-like appearance, made mainly of ice crystals, partly or totally covering the sky. Sun or moon are clearly visible through this kind of cloud, which clearly distinguishes it from altostratus. If the sun or moon is surrounded by a halo, the cloud is almost certainly cirrostratus. Often signals change in weather. If it forms from cirrus and grows thicker and more continuous, it may mean clouds and wet weather are on the way. If gaps begin to appear and it changes into cirrocumulus, the weather is probably going to remain fair and dry for several days.

Middle Clouds

The heights of medium-level cloud bases vary greatly according to the region over which they form. Changes in cloud temperature are affected by air temperature, latitude and time of day. There is less variety in these clouds than in low-level clouds, because the clouds are farther away from the influences of ground heating and cooling. What variety there is is difficult to see because they are so high in the sky.

Nimbostratus Clouds

From *nimbus* (rain) and *stratus* (sheet), these clouds are the source of gentle, but continuous, rain or snow. Nimbostratus is a dark, gray cloud blanket that is thick enough to hide the sun and any other higher clouds. These clouds form when warm, moist air is lifted steadily over a large area, usually at a warm front. (Made of water droplets, raindrops, snow crystals and snowflakes.)

Altostratus Clouds

Grayish or bluish, watery-looking fibrous or sheet cloud that partly or totally covers the sky and blocks out the sun in places. This cloud forms when the stable air behind a shallow-sloped warm front is lifted slowly over the steeper-sloped cold front that is overtaking it. Can bring rain or snow. (Made mainly of water droplets and ice crystals with some raindrops and snowflakes.)

Altocumulus (I and II) Clouds

Small, white, puffy cloudlets that look like dozens of little cotton balls, wave crests or tufted fragments. Usually forms in a layer of moist air, where air currents undulate gently like waves on the sea. As a wave rises, water vapor condenses and there is a cloud. In the wave troughs, water evaporates. There the cloud is thinner or the sky may be clear, producing bands of cloud. Or moist air is cooled by turbulence, then lifted up slightly and cooled to form a layer of cloud at that height. (Made mainly of water droplets.)

The bases of low-level clouds are often very shallow but others can reach 8 miles (13 km) high. The heights of low-level cloud bases vary according to the time of year, the latitude over which they form and the time of day. All of these factors affect the air temperature, which in turn affects the way that clouds form and the shape they take.

Stratus Clouds

Smooth and featureless. Fairly uniform gray cloud layer, often low enough to block out tops of low hills or high buildings. Often forms in stable air, which has little or no turbulence. Means rain when it forms over hilltops. (Made of small water droplets or ice particles at low temperatures.)

Stratocumulus Clouds

Meaning "sheets of lumpy cloud." Gray, white or a mixture of both, usually with darker patches. Shaped like rolls, waves or rounded masses. Form when warm, moist air mixes with drier, cooler air and the whole mixture moves beneath warmer lighter air. Looks threatening, but unless it is very thick usually produces only drizzle or light precipitation. Although not in itself a "bad weather cloud," it can indicate that bad weather is on the way or just clearing up. (Made of water droplets, sometimes raindrops or snow pellets, and more rarely snow crystals and snowflakes.)

Cumulus (I and II) Clouds

Meaning "heaped." Puffy white clouds of vertical development that are limited in horizontal growth. These clouds form in columns of rising air. Appear as separate clouds with sharp outlines "growing" upwards in rising mounds, domes or towers, with bulging upper parts that look like a cauliflower. Sunlit parts are brilliant white; bases are dark and flat. When small and scattered are indicators of fine weather. (Made of water droplets and ice crystals.)

Cumulonimbus (I and II) Clouds

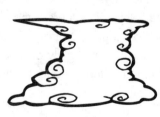

Dark, menacing, heavy, dense cloud like a mountain or huge tower, upper parts smooth and flattened spread out in a dark plume. Resembles cumulus cloud but towers much higher. Under the very dark base, low ragged clouds often form. These huge clouds can stand alone or sometimes form a wall. In these very violent clouds, rain falls and thunder and lightning are produced. Form on hot summer days with clear skies and no wind, when humid air rises as it becomes heated from contact with the ground. (Made of water droplets, ice crystals, large raindrops and often snowflakes, snow pellets, ice pellets or hailstones.)

Clouds made up mostly of water droplets have sharp, well-defined edges; while those that are made up of mostly ice crystals appear fuzzy and diffused.

Cloud Watchers

Cloud watching is a relaxing, fascinating and productive way to spend time on your back. It is amazing to see how much actually goes on above our heads and how quickly and often the picture changes.

Try This

To be a "cloud watcher" you must first find a dry spot to lie down on. Once on your back, look up and scan the sky (be careful not to look directly at the sun).

- What do the clouds look like? Are they high, low, thick and fluffy, stringy, white, gray, lumpy, fat and billowy, wispy and thin? Record your observations.

- Do you see any clouds with eyes, ears, snouts, arms, antlers or tails? How about animals – crocodiles, sheep, whales, dinosaurs – or strange alien creatures and their spaceships?

- Try to describe the different kinds of clouds you see by the shapes and objects they form.

- Choose one cloud and watch it continuously over the next few minutes. How has it changed? How fast is it moving?

- Back in the classroom, hold a discussion and find out who saw what.

Above the clouds the sun is always shining, and the sky is always blue.

Cotton Ball Clouds

Use cotton balls, glue and blue construction paper cloud cut-outs to make cumuliform, stratiform and cirriform clouds.

Materials

3 blue construction paper cloud shapes
glue
cotton balls

What to Do

1 To make a cirriform cloud, pull the cotton balls apart until they are thin and wispy. Glue onto the blue cloud shape.

2 To make a stratiform cloud, pull the cotton balls in all directions to flatten and lengthen. Glue onto the blue cloud shape in flat, even layers.

3 To make a cumuliform cloud, leave the cotton balls as they are. Glue onto the blue cloud shape in clusters or piles for a heaped effect.

Cloud Forecasters

Cut out and laminate the 10 cloud genera provided here. Choose a different cloud forecaster each day to determine what kind of clouds are present and then stick the corresponding laminate(s) on a classroom cloud calendar. These cloud forecasts should be taken several times over the course of one school day. (At the end of the day the teacher can draw the cloud types observed for a permanent record.)

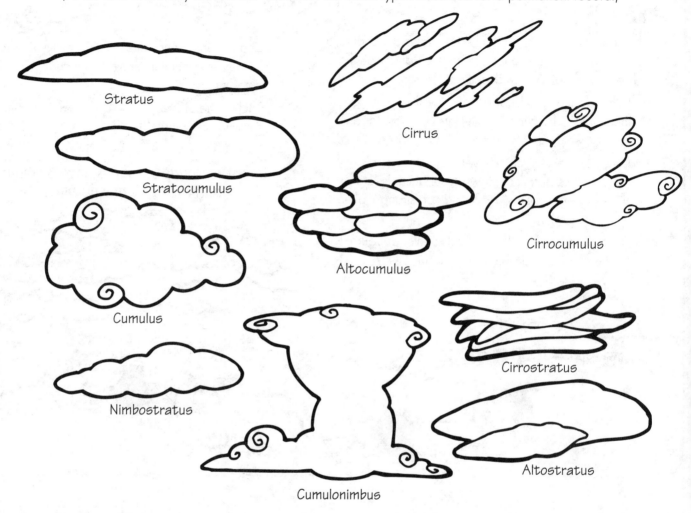

Students can have their own desktop version of the cloud calendar. Individual students can keep a running cloud record by drawing on their own calendars the different clouds posted each day on the classroom calendar.

Refer to your Weather Watch Calendar on page 12. Is it possible to predict the weather using the cloud forecast?

Vapor Trails

Airplanes flying at high altitudes make a line of cirrus clouds across the sky when the water vapor from their engines freezes into ice crystals in the cold air. These vapor trails–or condensation trails ("contrails")–look like long white tails. Sometimes these clouds spread across the sky, widening the cloud. We can use contrails to help us forecast the weather. If a contrail vanishes quickly, the weather will be good. If it lingers, a storm could be on the way.

TLC10072 Copyright © Teaching & Learning Company, Carthage, IL 62321-0010

Your Head Is in the Clouds

People who are idealistic or dreamers are said to have their head in the clouds. If you could make the impossible possible, what would you do? Write your ideas on the lined cloud cut-out and then post your cloud on the Head in the Clouds class bulletin board.

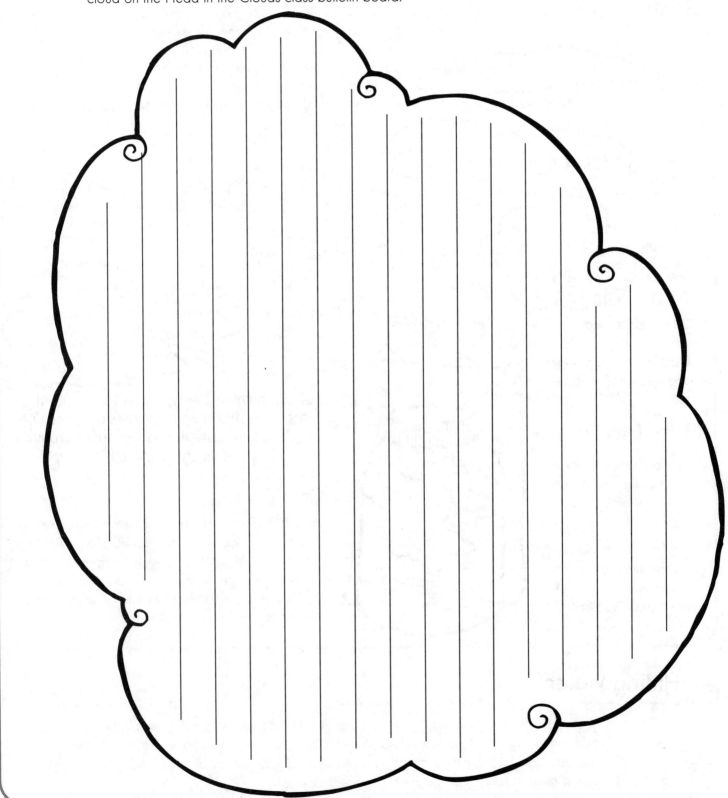

CCN–Cloud Condensation Nuclei

Super cooled water droplets are those that resist the temptation to change into ice crystals–even in clouds where temperatures are well below freezing.

There is more to most clouds than just water droplets and ice crystals. Under ordinary circumstances, water vapor must have something to cling to before it will condense, so it is a good thing that the air is not as clear as it looks. Tiny particles of dust, pollen, salt, soot and sulphate are floating around above our heads just waiting to be grabbed by a water droplet. When water vapor comes in contact with one of these particles, known as Cloud Condensation Nuclei or CCN, it condenses into the tiny, but visible, water droplets and ice crystals that are the building blocks of clouds.

There are one million CCN in every liter of air over water; five to six million over land!

Cloud Cling-Ons

You can see CCN at work by introducing particles into the air in a bottle.

Materials

2-liter plastic soda container (or other plastic bottle)
water
black construction paper
small plastic bag of ice
match

What to Do

1 Pour warm tap water into the plastic container until it is about ¹/₃ full.

2 Tape black paper to the back of the container (this will improve visibility).

3 Light a match, blow it out and quickly drop it into the container.

4 Immediately cover the mouth of the container with the bag of ice.

Clouds form as the warm water evaporates, rises, cools and then condenses onto the CCN, in this case the small pieces of dust introduced into the air by the match smoke.

Try This

• Put 2" (5 cm) of warm water in the plastic container. Instead of ice, screw the cap back on the bottle as soon as the match has been dropped into the bottle. Squeeze the bottle hard and rinse away any condensation that has formed. When the inside air is clear, release the bottle.

Hiding Water

You might not be able to see the water in the air, but it is there. On a summer day you could fill eight milk cartons with the water that is "hiding" in the air inside your classroom. This water has been "sucked" out of lakes, river and oceans-even puddles and laundry off the clothesline-by a process called *evaporation*.

Why Are Rain and Snow Clouds So Dark?

Rain and snow clouds are dark because they are filled with cloud droplets, rain droplets and ice crystals that are about to fall. The droplets and crystals block the sunlight from coming through the cloud. The more droplets and crystals, the less light that gets through and the darker the cloud. Really dark clouds contain a lot of snow, which blocks the light even more.

One instrument meteorologists use to determine if rain or snow is on the way is a "cloud gun." Radar towers "shoot" microwave beams into the sky to zap clouds. Although the beams pass through most clouds, they cannot pierce rain and snow clouds. The way beams bounce back off these clouds gives meteorologists advanced warning of bad weather.

 ## Every Cloud Has a Silver Lining

People who have a lot of bad luck are said to have a dark cloud hanging over them. But there is a bright spot in every cloud–even the darkest ones. That is what is meant by the expression "every cloud has a silver lining." and the advice to "look for the silver lining" There is something good to be found in every bad situation. Make your own "cloud with a silver lining."

Materials

2 white paper cloud cut-outs (one slightly larger than the other)
silver crayon, marker or paint (Silver glitter or glue-glitter can be used as a substitute.)

What to Do

1 Paint or color the edges of the larger white cloud cut-out with silver paint. Allow to dry.

2 On a plain cut-out, describe a bad situation. (For example: My mother got remarried, and I don't get to spend much time alone with her anymore.)

3 On the silver-edged cut-out describe something good that could come out of the bad situation. (For example: I have a new stepbrother to play with!)

4 Staple the two clouds together at the top with a single staple.

5 Suspend the clouds from a mobile or the ceiling, or tack onto a bulletin board.

73

Chapter 6
Rainy Weather

Even though we can't always see it, there is water in the air all around us. Sometimes it is visible as rain; sometimes we feel it as humidity. The air soaks up water and because there is water in the air, we have different types of weather.

The human body is 2/3 water!
We are losing the water from our bodies all the time,
through sweating, breathing and . . . going to the bathroom!
To replace this water and stay healthy, people must drink water every day.
No one can survive more than four days without water.

Why Does It Rain?

As the heat of the sun warms the water in the oceans, lakes, rivers and even puddles, some of the water changes from a liquid to a gas. This gas is called *water vapor.* Because the gas is invisible, we can't see the water vapor, but it is there.

The warm air rises and draws the water vapor into the sky. The warmer the air, the more water vapor it can hold. As the warm air meets colder air higher in the sky, it cools. The colder the air, the less water vapor it can hold. Whenever there is more water in the air than the temperature will allow it to hold, the water vapor condenses—or changes back from a gas to a liquid. The liquid form of water vapor is water droplets. When congregations of these tiny water droplets come together, they form a cloud.

There are millions, billions even trillions of water droplets in a rain cloud. The average size thundercloud holds more than six trillion of them. These droplets are so small they float in the air. As the air continues to cool, they bump together and stick together, forming larger drops. These drops stay in the clouds, bumping and growing until they are too large and too heavy to float. Then they fall to the ground as rain.

There are about 15 million droplets of water vapor in one raindrop.

If the water drops are contained in very high clouds, they stick to tiny ice particles and freeze, making heavier ice crystals and snowflakes. If these flakes drop down through warmer air, they melt and fall as rain or drizzle. In the winter, when the air is cold right down to the ground, there is no chance for them to melt. Instead, they fall to the Earth as snow, freezing rain or hail!

Scientists estimate that 40 million gallons of water
–in the form of rain, snow or freezing rain–
fall on the Earth every second of every day!

Stormy Senses

Go outside during a rainstorm (not a thunderstorm!). Ask children what they smell, taste, hear, see and feel. Back in the classroom, write these sensations down. Use similes to make connections between stormy weather and other events in the lives of the children.

For example:

I smell	the Earth	like	when I water the garden	.
I taste	fresh air	like	when I am sitting by a lake	.
I hear	the sound of rain	like	wind swishing in the tall grass	.
I see	gray sky	like	my room just before dark	.
I feel	sad	like	when my best friend has gone away	.

I smell _____ **like** _____ .

I taste _____ **like** _____ .

I hear _____ **like** _____ .

I see _____ **like** _____ .

I feel _____ **like** _____ .

Homemade Raindrops

Materials

electric kettle
tin can filled with ice
pair of tongs
oven mitt

What to Do

1 Fill the kettle halfway with water and plug it in.

2 When the kettle is boiling, use the tongs to hold the tin full of ice over the steam. Wear the oven mitt to hold the tongs.

The drops that form and fall are rain! The water in the kettle evaporates and becomes steam, then collects at the bottom of the tin where the air is cool. The individual drops stick together, or "bond," to form larger drops, until they are heavy enough to fall.

Try This

• Put a small mirror in the freezer for about one hour. Take it out and breathe on it until it fogs over. What you see on the mirror is rain! Keep breathing on the mirror. See if you can make your "raindrops" collide and merge. Watch them run down the mirror bumping into one another, falling faster and faster as they get bigger and heavier.

The Earth is an expert at recycling. From the beginning of time, it has been using the same water over and over again. In fact, we are drinking the very water that the dinosaurs drank millions of years ago! Water moves between the sea, the atmosphere and the land in a continuous, three-part cycle we call the water, or "hydrological," cycle.

Although 70% of the Earth's surface is covered by huge oceans and seas and another 10% by ice, little new water is ever made on Earth.

One inch of rain over one square mile weighs 72,000 tons.

The Water Cycle

The rain that falls from the sky is part of an endless cycle: it has fallen billions of times before, and it will fall billions of times again.

Part 1: Evaporation

The sun's heat draws moisture up into the air as water vapor.

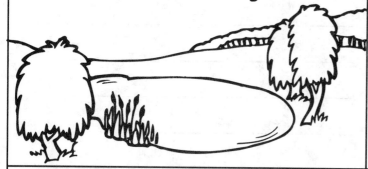

Part 2: Condensation

As the water vapor rises, it cools and condenses into tiny water droplets. The little droplets form clouds.

Part 3: Precipitation

The clouds meet cool air. The droplets merge together to form large, heavy drops and fall to the Earth as rain. When it is very cold, the drops fall as snow, freezing rain or hail. Much of this "water" eventually flows back into the world's oceans, seas and lakes.

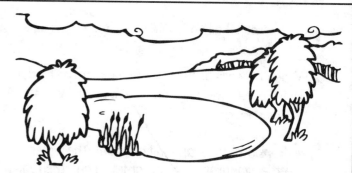

It takes about nine days for water to evaporate from the oceans or the surface of the Earth, condense as part of a cloud and fall to Earth again as rain or snow.

Blow Dryer

Try putting a little water on a tissue (be careful not to soak it!) or on your arm. Blow on the tissue (or your skin) for a few minutes. What happens to the water?

The "wind" of your breath heats up the water and changes it to water vapor.

The water has evaporated, leaving the tissue (and you!) dry.

Be an Evaporation Detective

Like humans, plants release water into the air. Usually, the evaporation process is invisible: water escapes from plants into the air as water vapor and eventually ends up as water droplets and then raindrops in a storm cloud. With the aid of a plastic bag, however, you can solve the mystery of the missing water.

Materials

small potted plant
plastic bag
twist-tie or piece of string
sunny windowsill

What to Do

1 Place the entire plant in a plastic bag.

2 Carefully tie the bag so it is tightly sealed.

3 Place the plant in the windowsill.

After 24 hours you will notice water drops collecting on the inside of the plastic bag. This is the water that has evaporated from the tiny pores in the leaves of the plant and then condensed on the cool plastic.

Mouth Clouds: A Lesson in Condensation

Have you ever noticed that you can see your breath in the winter but not in the summer? This is because warm air can hold a great deal of water and cold air cannot. When you breathe out, or exhale, on a hot day, the moisture in your breath disperses easily in the air. On cold days, however, the air cannot hold all the water in your breath. The vapor condenses and makes a little cloud.

77

Finger Puppet Rain Play

Cut out and color these figures. Tape to make finger puppets. Perform a cause-and-effect rain play. Use a rain mobile as a fitting backdrop.

The Naming Game

Rain is the name that is given to falling water droplets that measure more than $1/50$" (0.1 mm) across. Droplets that are smaller than this can still be called rain if there are wide spaces between them, but smaller droplets that fall close together are called drizzle. It is easy to tell the difference between raindrops and drizzle: raindrops make a tiny splash when they fall into a puddle; drizzle droplets do not. Small raindrops can fall as fast as 29.5' (9 m) per second. That is as fast as you can pedal your bicycle!

A single raindrop may contain as many as one million water droplets before it is heavy enough to fall back to the Earth.

Size Wise

Raindrops come in a variety of sizes. Some are five times larger than others. Like pizzas, there are four main size classifications for raindrops:

Small: $1/13$" (2 mm)
Medium: $1/8$" (3 mm)
Large: $1/4$" (6 mm)
Extra Large: $1/3$" (1 cm)

A giant raindrop, $1/3$" (1 cm), across – about the width of a pencil – once fell in Hawaii.

The Shape of Things

Everyone knows that raindrops are shaped like teardrops, right? Wrong! Believe it or not, falling raindrops actually look like miniature pancakes. They start out round, but the wind resistance they encounter on the way down flattens them.

Raindrop Art

Raindrop Prints

See what raindrops look like when they hit the ground.

Materials

shallow pan
flour
craft stick
sieve
bowl
rainy day

What to Do

1 Pour about $1/2$" (1.25 cm) of flour into the pan.

2 Level the surface of the flour with a craft stick.

3 Put the pan out in the rain until the flour is spattered with raindrops.

4 Return to the classroom and pour the flour through the sieve.

The lumps that remain in your sieve are raindrop prints!

Try This

• Measure the raindrops you caught with a ruler. How big are they?
Are they all the same size?
Are the raindrop prints all the same shape?
Can you draw them?

Sketch a Raindrop

When you look at a raindrop, what do you see? Use a sketch pad and pencil to sketch raindrops in the air, as they hit a surface and as they settle on it.

Trace a Raindrop

Let a raindrop fall on your paper. Trace it with a pencil or a marker and watch the colors bleed into and mix with the water.

How Many Raindrops?

Enjoy this estimate, multiply and discover activity.

Materials

¹/₄ teaspoon (1.25 ml)
eyedropper
water

Sample Questions

1 Use the eyedropper to determine how many water droplets are in ¹/₄ teaspoon (1.25 ml).

2 How many water droplets would there be in ¹/₂ teaspoon (2.5 ml)?

3 Do you need to use the eyedropper to find out? (Hint: ¹/₂ teaspooon [2.5 ml] is twice as large as ¹/₄ teaspoon [1.25 ml].)

4 How many water droplets would there be in 1 teaspoon? (Hint: There are four ¹/₄ teaspoons [1.25 ml] and two ¹/₂ teaspoons [2.5 ml] in 1 teaspoon [5 ml].)

5 If there are 3 teaspoons in a tablespoon, how many droplets would there be in one tablespoon (15 ml)?

6 If there are 16 tablespoons in a cup, how many droplets would there be in one cup (240 ml)?

Colored Rain

Rain is not always clear and colorless. Red, black and green rains have all been recorded by scientists in various parts of the world. Rain becomes colored when water droplets pick up bits of colored dust or pollen as they fall.

 ## Measuring Rain

Meteorologists use a rain gauge to measure rainfall. Make your own school yard rain gauge.

Materials

narrow, sturdy tin can
small block of wood
ruler
open area outside
rainy day

What to Do

1 Place the tin can on a block of wood so that it is level.

2 Place the block in an open area. (To get a true rainfall reading, your rain gauge must be out in the open, away from the school, trees or fences.)

3 Make sure the top of the open can is about 12" (30 cm) above the ground.

4 Immediately after a rainstorm–before any water has had a chance to evaporate–lower a ruler into the can and measure how much water it contains. (This will tell you how much rain has fallen.)

5 Empty the can and put it back on the block of wood in the same open place.

6 Back in the classroom, record that number on a "rain date calendar." (If the amount of rainwater collected is too small to measure, mark *T* for *Trace* on your calendar.)

Questions to Ask

- Did your classmates record the same measurement?

- Check the local paper to find out the official rainfall. Was your rain gauge accurate?

- See how much rain falls in a day/week/month. Include these figures on your Weather Watch Calendar (page 12).

 ## Uneven Rain

If you and your classmates did not come up with the same numbers in the rain gauge exercise, it might not be the result of "human error." Rain does not fall evenly. To see for yourself, place six tin cans of the same size in various positions around the school yard (near the school wall, under the drip-line of a tree, in the middle of the school yard, by a play structure, under a shrub, etc.).

After a rainfall, take a measuring cup and measure the amount of water collected in each container. Chances are, the measurements will not all be the same.

Try This

- To get the average measurement, collect all the water in another can. Then use your ruler to measure the total. Divide that number by six (the number of can collectors).

The Wettest . . .

Mount Waialeale in Kauai in the Hawaiian Islands is the wettest place on Earth. It gets an average of 460" (27 m)-more than 38' (11.5 m)!-of rain every year. That is enough to cover a three-story building. It also has the most rainy days each year-335 to 350. (With only 365 days in a year, that means Mount Waialeale might only have 15 rain-free days!)

and the Most

- India is the proud record holder for the most rainfall ever to fall in one year: 1,044" (26,518 mm). That is 87' (27 m) of water and an average of 2.9" (7.3 cm) of rain a day!
- On July 4, 1956, 1.22" (31 mm) of rain fell in Unionville, Maryland, in one minute! If it had rained that hard for an hour, the water would have been over people's heads.
- One day in 1952, 73.62" (1.87 m) of rain-more than 6' (1.82 m)!-fell on Cilaos, in the Indian Ocean. That is the most rain ever to fall in a 24-hour period.

It rains almost every day in tropical rain forests.

. . . to the Driest

The driest place in the world is the Atacama Desert in Chile. It gets less than 0.02" (0.50 mm) of rain each year. The Atacama Desert is also the location of the longest drought, which lasted 400 years, and of a dusty little town called Arica, which went for 14 years straight without a single drop of rain!

and the Least

- No rain ever falls in Antarctica and only 4" to 6" (10 to 15 cm) of new snow coats the continent each year. (Oddly enough, more fresh water is locked up in the ice in Antarctica than can be found in the rest of the world's freshwater resources combined!)
- Little rain ever falls over the world's hot desert areas. The reason: the air is too warm for clouds to form.

On farms in the hottest regions of Australia, precious rainwater is stored in open tanks. These tanks sound like prime targets for heavy-duty water loss, but in fact, the opposite is true.

A layer of white balls floating on the surface of the water allows rain to enter the barrel but reflects sunlight, diminishing evaporation.

Rainmaker

In this follow-the-leader activity, children become more aware of what happens before, during and after a rainstorm.

Materials

Have the children sit in a circle. (A hard floor surface works best, but carpet will do.) The teacher leads and is copied by the first child, who is copied by the second child, who is copied by the third child and so on around the circle. (Because following can be a difficult task for little ones, reinforce the concept by having each child point to the person he or she will copy.)

Make sure the children understand that not everyone will be doing the same thing at the same time. Each child is to watch the person he or she is to copy - not the teacher!

To Start

The teacher gently, slowly, taps two fingers together. When the last student has joined in, the teacher then continues tapping and gently blows to imitate a soft wind. When the last student has joined in, the teacher then blows a little louder and snaps fingers.

The teacher then continues blowing and rubs palms together to make a swishing sound.

Then blows and slaps hands on floor to imitate the sound of large raindrops falling.

Then continues blowing and rubs palms together to make a swishing sound.

Then continues blowing and slapping and stamps feet in a roll of thunder. (This is very exciting and the climax of the storm!)

Then continues blowing and slapping but stops stamping feet. (The storm has begun to subside.)

Then blows and slaps more gently.

Then rubs hands together gently and blows lightly.

Then taps fingers and blows lightly.

Then taps fingers very slowly and stops blowing.

Then folds hands on lap and sits very quietly. (The storm has passed.)

Rainy Day Word Play

As a class, brainstorm to come up with a list of rain words (such as: *slosh, mud, spatter, splatter, umbrella, rain, drip, drop, splash, splish, downpour, shower*). Write these words on the chalkboard. Have students write stories or poems using the words from your list.

Indian Rain Symbols

Long ago, North American Native Americans used picture symbols to depict rain and other events associated with wet weather. In very dry areas, the Native Americans put these symbols on their clothing, blankets, tepees, headdresses and other important articles to attract the rain.

Among these symbols were those that represented such beliefs as:

- lightning strikes the four corners of the Earth
- the Sacred Mountains are the home of the spirits who bring rain
- rain clouds bring gentle rain to crops
- faraway clouds over mountains can bring rain the following day
- a rainbow comes after a good rain

In Native American cultures, the rainmakers were people who claimed they could make it rain by singing secret incantations, performing special rain dances or using a variety of magic potions.

Rain

Rain Clouds

Thunder and Lightning

Sun

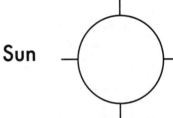

Rain Rituals

The Rain Dance

In religious rituals, dance is a way of thanking the gods or asking for their help. For a dance to be successful, it is critical that the steps are always performed in the same order.

The Hopi Indians believe that rain is brought by spirits called Kachinas. To attract the attention of the Kachinas, Hopi dance in special clothing and dress dolls to look like the lead dancer responsible for calling the spirits.

Try This

- Make up your own rain dance. Choose a leader. Everyone follows the actions of the leader. Perform the rain dance as a class. (Change leaders often.)

Puddle Jumping

There are other rain rituals. In North America, puddle jumping is such a popular children's pastime that it could be considered a ritual! The steps are easy to learn and pretty much the same anywhere you go, and the "special clothing"-rubber boots-is standard fare!

Rubber Boot Scramble

This is a hilarious, problem-solving group activity.

Materials

circle of children
as many pairs of rubber boots (labeled) as there are
    kids, placed in a pile
dry floor to sit on

What to Do

1 Form a large circle of players around the pile of
rubber boots.

2 Have one player "stir up" the boots until they are
well scrambled.

3 Have each player pick and put on two unmatched
boots that do not belong to them.

4 Keeping the boots on their feet, have children
reunite the pairs and reform the circle with each pair
of boots matched. (i.e. the child with Sally's boot
on the left foot and Sam's boot on the right will
have, to her left, the child with Sally's other boot
on the right foot and, to her right, the child with Sam's
other boot on the left foot.)

5 Return the boots to the pile and then reunite with
their owners.

Try This

- Like Duck-Duck-Goose, have one player walk
around the circle and tap another player on the
shoulder. Both players enter the circle, find and put
on their own pair of boots, then race back to their
spots in the circle.

- Choose two students to race against one another.
The first one to dress in the correct boots and sit in
the circle is the winner.

- At random, choose a student to enter the circle
and, as quickly as possible, find and get into their
own boots. Have the others count to see how long
the player takes to get his or her boots on. (This
can be a "who is fastest" game.) When that student is sitting, choose another player. Play continues until all boots have owners!

- Have all students enter the circle at the same time
and find their own boots. The first one back to the
circle wearing the right boots is the winner.

- Same as above only class is divided into teams.

Rainy Day Cut-Outs

Color and cut out these paper kids and clothes. Then "dress" the kids accordingly, pasting, taping or tabbing on the appropriate rainy day attire.

Try This

- String your rainy day kids together and hang from the walls or ceiling for decoration.

Q: What do you get when you go for a walk in the rain?

A: Wet!

Q: What happens when it rains cats and dogs?

A: You step in a poodle!

Q: What did the dirt say to the rain?

A: If you keep that up, my name will be mud!

Q: Why do people carry umbrellas when it rains?

A: Because umbrellas can't walk!

Q: What can go through water without getting wet?

A: Sunlight

Q: What's worse than raining cats and dogs?

A: Hailing taxis.

Q: What do you get when you cross a rainstorm with a small dog?

A: A poodle.

Betcha Challenge

I'll betcha I can stay underwater for two hours.
(When you are challenged, hold a glass of water over your head!)

Weather-Related Knock-Knock Jokes

Knock-knock.
  Who's there?
Olive.
  Olive who?
"Olive" the rain.

Knock-knock.
  Who's there?
Ethan.
  Ethan who?
"Ethan" it great?

Knock-knock.
  Who's there?
Aldo.
  Aldo who?
"Aldo" anything to go for a walk in the rain.

Knock-knock.
  Who's there?
Ken.
  Ken who?
"Ken" I go splash in it?

Knock-knock.
  Who's there?
Howard.
  Howard who?
"Howard" you like to come?

Knock-knock.
  Who's there?
Adam.
  Adam who?
"Adam" my way; I'm coming!

Knock-knock.
  Who's there?
Les.
  Les who?
"Les" grab our umbrellas, first.

Knock-knock.
  Who's there?
Omar.
  Omar who?
"Omar" goodness, am I ever wet!

Knock-knock.
  Who's there?
Doris.
  Doris who?
"Doris" a lot of rain in that puddle.

Knock-knock.
  Who's there?
Emma.
  Emma who?
"Emma" 'fraid of thunderstorms!

Knock-knock.
  Who's there?
Phil
  Phil who?
"Phil" like splashing in the rain with me?

Knock-knock.
  Who's there?
Hugh.
  Hugh who?
"Hugh" better get inside then.

Knock-knock.
  Who's there?
Luke.
  Luke who?
"Luke" out! There's a thunderstorm!

Knock-knock.
  Who's there?
Justin.
  Justin who?
"Justin" time. I hear thunder.

Fun-in-the-Rain Play Day

Rainy days are a sensory wonderland. The trouble is, few of us ever get to enjoy them. Getting the kids out in the rain for a rainy play day is a great way to sharpen the senses and have fun at the same time. Here are some ideas to make your Fun-in-the-Rain Play Day an unqualified success.

Nose Drops

Tip your head back and look up into the rain. Count the number of drops that hit your nose in one minute.

Raindrop Roundup

Materials

1 cup for each player
2 measuring cups, sheltered from the rain

What to Do

1 Divide the class into two teams.

2 Give a cup to each player.

3 Have the players hold their cups upside down until they are told to "Go!"

4 Players try to catch as many raindrops in their cups as possible, then pour them into their team measuring cup.

5 At the "Stop!" command, players must stop adding water to their measuring cups.

6 Compare measuring cups. The team with the most rain collected is the winner!

Outdoor (or Indoor) Rain Center

At last, a real water center! This is a wonderful activity for a warm, rainy day (as long as everyone is prepared in advance and has a dry set of clothes to change into after the fun!). Set up several water play tables outside. Include buckets, cups, tubs, spray bottles, sponges, sieves, funnels, straws, tubes, shaving cream, ice cubes, soap, food coloring (with adult supervision only!) and anything else that catches your fancy.

Try This

- Punch holes in the bottom of several milk cartons. Fill with water and hold overhead. Watch it rain . . . even more!

90

Singing in the Rain

What better place to sing rainy day songs than out in the weather that inspired their creation? There is nothing like a choir in the rain, and the raindrops add natural rhythm! Here is a short collection to set your toes a-tapping and your hands a-clapping "weather" you are under the clouds or the fluorescent lights.

Rainy Day Songs and Rhymes

Rain Cloud, Rain Cloud, in the Sky

(To the tune of "Twinkle, Twinkle, Little Star")
Rain cloud, rain cloud, up so high,
Drop your raindrops from the sky.
Let them fall upon the ground,
And I'll go dancing all around.
Rain cloud, rain cloud, up so high,
Drop your raindrops from the sky.

Rain on the Green Grass

Rain on the green grass,
Rain on the sea.
Rain on the housetops,
But not on me!

Pull on Your Mackintosh*

Pull on your rubber boots
And your yellow mackintosh.
The puddles are waiting
For you to splash and splosh.

*The mackintosh was the first waterproof raincoat ever invented.

Rain, Rain, Go Away

Rain, rain, go away,
Come again another day.
Little (child's name) wants to play,
Rain, rain, go away.

Raindrop, Raindrop

(To the tune of "Baa, Baa, Black Sheep")
Raindrop, raindrop,
Pudgy little fella,
I'll get my boots and my umbrella.
Then I'll jump and splash about,
Just until the sun comes out.
Raindrop, raindrop,
Pudgy little fella,
I'll get my boots and my umbrella.

It's Raining;
It's Pouring

It's raining;
It's pouring;
The old man is snoring.
Bumped his head,
And he went to bed,
And he didn't get up 'til the morning.

Slip on Your Raincoat

Slip on your raincoat.
Pull on your galoshes.
Wading in puddles,
Makes splishes and sploshes.

Hot Water/Cold Water

Hot water,
Cold water,
Running down your back water.
(Tap the child's shoulders rhythmically and then tickle down the back.)

Raindrops, Raindrops

Raindrops, raindrops!
Falling all around.
(Move fingers to imitate falling rain)
Pitter-patter on the rooftops.
(Tap fingers softly on head)
Pitter-patter on the ground.
(Tap fingers softly on feet or floor)
Here is my umbrella.
(Pretend to open umbrella)
It will keep me dry.
(Hold umbrella over head)
When I go walking in the rain,
I hold it up so high.
(Lift umbrella high in air)

**Some people think it is bad luck
–not to mention dangerous–
to open an umbrella inside!**

Parent Notice

To ensure the success of your Fun-in-the-Rain Play Day, send home a note in advance advising parents that you will be venturing outside for some rain play on the next fair/foul day. Ask them to send in a bag for their child that contains a towel, a spare set of clothes and a favorite water toy. Make sure parents understand that these articles might have to remain at school for a few days or even weeks until the weather cooperates.

Name _____

Rainy Day Seatwork

Raindrop Matchup

Draw a line to connect each raindrop pair.

Connect the Raindrops

Connect the raindrops to reveal some rainy day essentials.

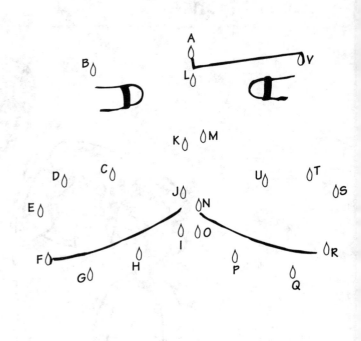

Make a Rain Mobile

Materials

scissors
crayons/markers
hole punch
string (seven pieces of varying lengths)
2 straws

What to Do

1 Cut out. and color both sides of these five rainy day objects.

2 Cut out and punch a hole in the top of each object.

3 Thread a piece of string through each hole and knot.

4 Tie one piece of string to the middle of both straws.

5 Tie another piece of string to the top straw.

6 Tie rainy day objects to the two straws: two on the top straw, three on the bottom.

7 Hang mobiles from the ceiling.

Rain Delay Activity Page

Rain affects our lives in many ways. Sometimes it even prevents us from doing certain things. Circle the activities you cannot continue in the rain. Color the activities that continue and are unaffected (assuming there is no threat of a thunderstorm).

Rainbows

Of all of the results of weather, rainbows are perhaps the most beautiful. Rainbows occur naturally at the tail end of a rainstorm or during a sun shower, when the sun shines through raindrops in the air at just the right angle.

"Bow" Watching

To see a rainbow, you have to have your back to the sun. This means that the best times for rainbow watching are early in the day or late in the afternoon, when the sun is not directly overhead but sitting low on the horizon. The clearest rainbows are visible on days when the raindrops in the air are large. If conditions are excellent, you might even see a double rainbow!

You can also watch for two other "bows." Moonbows can be seen after the rain when a full moon has just risen. The key ingredients, as with fogbows (when sunlight shines through fog), are water droplets in the air and light.

Why a Rainbow?

Sunlight is made up of seven beams of color: red, orange, yellow, green, blue, indigo and violet. Although we cannot usually see these colors, they are always there. Together, these beams are called the *spectrum*. When sunlight hits raindrops at a certain angle, the white beam bends and its seven composite colors, formerly blended together, are split apart. These colors form a rainbow in a breathtaking arc across the sky.

Rainbows actually occur in circular bands,
but because we see the top part of the band only,
the rainbow appears as an arc across the Earth.

Each of the colors of the spectrum has a different wavelength: red is the longest; violet is the shortest. When white light is split apart and forms a rainbow, the colors of the spectrum always appear in the same order: (R)ed, (O)range, (Y)ellow, (G)reen, (B)lue, (I)ndigo and (V)iolet, or ROYGBIV.

Remembering the Spectrum

To help students remember the order of the colors of the rainbow, have them make up clever sentences using the letters of ROYGBIV in the order of their appearance. Write the letters on the chalkboard and give them an example, such as: Rain On Your Grass Brings Interesting Variety. After students have devised their own sentences, read them aloud. Have the class vote on which is easiest to remember. Write this phrase on the chalkboard and have students incorporate the most popular phrase in a rainbow picture.

Spectrum Tag

Choose one person to be the sun (IT). All other players are raindrops. When the sun touches a raindrop, it gives the raindrop a color and asks it to stand against the wall as part of the ROYGBIV spectrum. Once seven players have been captured by the sun and can sound off their colors in order, a new sun is chosen.

Send a letter home to parents explaining that you are teaching the students about rainbows and the seven colors of the spectrum. Request that students dress in the color of the rainbow circled on their letter on a specific date. (Make sure all colors are well represented.) Have the children line up according to their clothing and their place on the spectrum. Take a picture of your clothing rainbow!

Create Your Own Rainbow

Make a rainbow in the classroom.

Materials

pocket mirror
glass bowl
flashlight
white wall (or a piece
of white paper)

What to Do

When the bowl is half full of water, rest the mirror against its side at a 45° angle. Shine the flashlight beam directly down on the mirror from overhead and look for the rainbow on the wall opposite. Have students trace the rainbow with ROYGBIV colors.

- Use sunlight instead of a flashlight. Move the mirror around in the water at different angles until the rainbow becomes visible.

- Fill a jar with water and place it on a sunny, classroom windowsill. Move white paper next to the jar until the bright colors of the rainbow are reflected on it.

- Hold a mirror with a beveled edge in a beam of sunlight (or flashlight beam). Move the mirror around until the rainbow is projected onto a wall.

- Use a prism to split the white light from a flashlight into its seven color bands.

Rainbow Wheel

Materials

jam jar lid
piece of white cardboard
pencil
ruler
colored pencils
scissors
length of wool

What to Do

1 Draw a circle on the cardboard following the outline of the jam jar.

2 Divide the circle into seven equal parts and color each part in one of the colors of the rainbow. (Follow ROYGBIV.)

3 Repeat this on the other side of the cardboard making sure to match the colors.

4 Poke two small holes just to the right and left of the center of the circle.

5 Thread the wool through both holes and knot the ends.

6 Hold one end of the loop in each hand and "wind up" your string by swinging the circle over and over.

7 Move your hands together and apart to set the rainbow wheel spinning.

The colors will blend together and become white. Because the wheel is spinning so fast, your eyes can no longer see each color separately, and your brain thinks there are no colors at all!

Stick-On Rainbow

Materials

paper rainbow on this sheet
glue
small container for glue
rice, pasta, eggshells, crumpled crepe paper, shredded
   construction paper or any other appropriate material that can be divided into the seven different colors
   of the rainbow
scissors
string

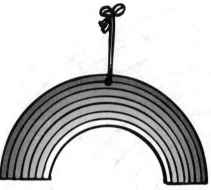

What to Do

1 Dip your finger in the glue.

2 Spread the glue from left to right across one band of the rainbow.

3 Then sprinkle with colored sand, rice, pasta, eggshells, crumpled crepe paper, shredded construction paper (or any other appropriately colored material) according to the color indicated on the band. For best results, allow glue to dry between bands.

4 Cut out your rainbow.

5 Punch a hole in the top and thread string through. Tie a knot.

6 Hang your rainbow from the ceiling.

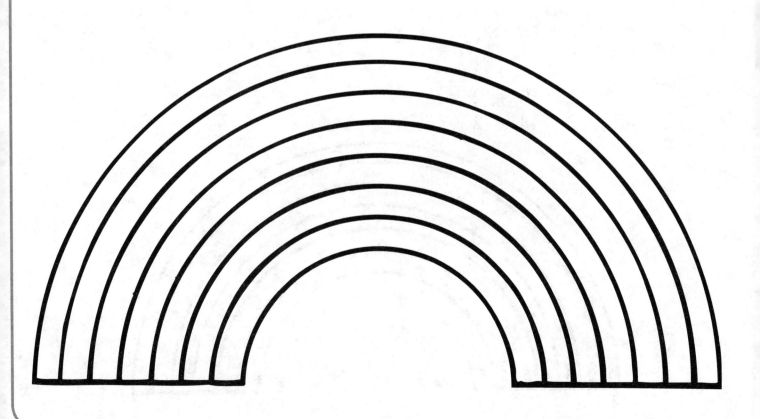

Rainbow Color-by-Number

Color Key:

1 = red, 2 = orange, 3 = yellow, 4 = green, 5 = blue, 6 = indigo, 7 = violet

Solve the equation for each segment and color the rainbow according to the color key.

5 − 3 =	0 + 2 =
6 − 3 =	1 + 3 =
7 − 2 =	3 + 3 =
10 − 3 =	

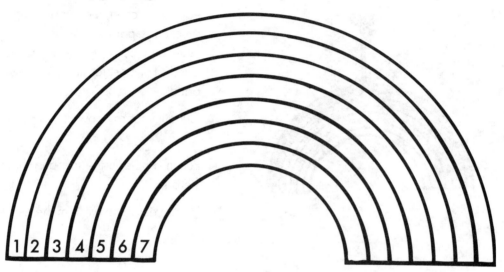

Solve the equation for each segment and color the rainbow according to the color key.

1 ÷ 1 =	2 x 1 =
9 ÷ 3 =	2 x 2 =
10 ÷ 2 =	3 x 2 =
14 ÷ 2 =	

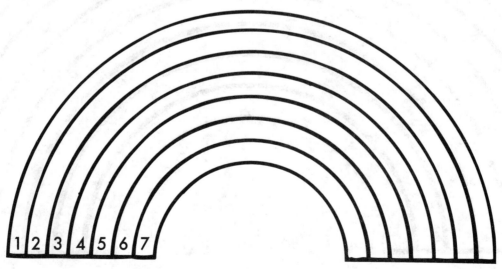

The Leprechaun's Treasure

Rainbows have fascinated humankind since the beginning of recorded history. Many tales have been created to explain the source and purpose of these beautiful bridges in the sky, but perhaps the most popular is the legend of the pot of gold at the end of the rainbow. It is said that any person who successfully follows the arc of the rainbow to the place where it touches the ground will find the elusive leprechaun's precious pot of gold.

Rainbow Maze

Follow the path to the pot of gold at the end of this rainbow.

101

Name _____

Rainy Day

Find each of the words listed at the bottom and circle in the puzzle. They can be found up, down, backwards and diagonally.

```
N  U  S  D  M  O  Y  F  U  N
H  A  T  E  L  D  D  U  P  S
T  O  O  B  D  S  P  O  R  D
H  E  R  U  M  W  A  T  E  R
U  U  M  B  R  E  L  L  A  I
N  O  Y  N  O  T  O  I  A  P
D  L  I  G  H  T  N  I  N  G
E  T  A  R  O  P  A  V  E  S
R  A  I  N  B  O  W  H  E  A
```

rain	umbrella	water	boot	drops	puddle
thunder	muddy	wet	sun	rainbow	fun
lightning	evaporate	stormy	drip	hat	

TLC10072 Copyright © Teaching & Learning Company, Carthage, IL 62321-0010

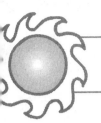

Chapter 7
Windy Weather

Simply stated, wind is the movement of the air around us. Wind is created when air flows from an area of high atmospheric pressure to an area of lower atmospheric pressure. The greater the difference between the two pressures, the stronger the wind will be. We know this today. But long ago people thought that the gods, not the atmosphere, created winds. Some people thought that winds were created by a god who squeezed a great bellows in the sky; others thought the gods kept winds hidden in a cave. In Japan, it was believed that a god named Fu Jin possessed a huge bag of wind. If Fu Jin opened the bag ever-so-slightly, a light wind would blow. If he opened the bag completely, however, the winds would blow at gale force.

Wind is never still.
If it were, it wouldn't be a wind;
it would be calm air.

Winds are belts of moving air that flow from one area to another driven by the "engine" of the sun. Currents are produced by the change in warm daytime air and cool night air. Because warm air is lighter than cold air, air warmed by the sun rises and creates an area of low pressure. Cooler, heavier air sweeps in to take its place. This creates a circular current . . . which produces winds. At night the air becomes cooler. The cool air falls, again creating a low-pressure area that must be filled. It is this cycle of heating and cooling that causes the air to move and winds to blow.

Air is always on the move and when air moves, it moves other things. Every day, everywhere we go, air is in action: it carries bubbles and dandelion seeds on the breeze, it blows flags and streamers in the wind, it moves the leaves in the trees and the smoke from your chimney; it lifts kites high in the air and it pushes people around on blustery days.

Make Your Own Wind

Try fanning yourself with a piece of paper. Do you feel anything on your skin? Of course! You have just created a wind. As the fan pushes the air out of its way, more air rushes in to take its place and, TA-DA!–wind. All that air moving over and around your skin makes you feel cool on a hot day and colder on a cold day.

Wind Worms

Materials

this paper
scissors
tape
string
wind

What to Do

1 Cut along the line of the spiral on this page to make a curly worm.

2 Tape a piece of string to the worm's head (at the center of the spiral).

3 Hold the end of the string in a gentle breeze.

Questions to Ask

• What happens to the worm? (It spins or spirals like a corkscrew.)

Try This

• Watch what happens to an inchworm on a breezy day when it repels down through the branches of a tree on its silky thread. Do both wind worms behave in the same way?

Windward Ho?

Air always flows from areas of higher pressure to areas of lower pressure . . . unless it gets bumped off course. But what could possibly change the direction of the wind? The Earth's spinning for one thing. The Earth's rotation adds a curve to the regular flow of air, creating a gentle spiral that twists inward. It forces the winds to turn right in the Northern Hemisphere and left in the Southern Hemisphere. Mountains, buildings and forests can change the direction of the wind, too, just like placing a stick in a stream changes the flow of water over and around it.

Wind funnels are created by valleys or canyons. As winds blow through these bottlenecks, their speeds increase and air pressure may fall. In cities, streets lined with tall buildings create the same effect and are referred to as "urban canyons."

104

Wind Varieties

Although you cannot feel the difference between them, there are literally hundreds of different kinds of winds. These fall into three main types: local winds, seasonal winds and prevailing winds. Local winds change according to air currents and local weather conditions. Seasonal winds, or monsoons, change direction with the seasons and often bring radical changes in weather. Prevailing winds are winds that always blow.

Sailors used to rely heavily on prevailing winds to carry their sailing ships across the oceans of the world.

Prevailing Winds

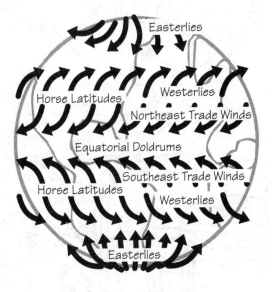

Prevailing winds are the biggest and most consistent winds on Earth. They blow thousands of miles year round. There are three main belts of prevailing winds on each side of the equator: trade winds (northeast and southeast), westerlies and polar easterlies. In addition to these, there are two other prevailing winds: the horse latitudes and the equatorial doldrums. Although wind direction changes daily according to shifting patterns of high and low pressures and vary according to the changing seasons, this system of prevailing winds circulates in a regular pattern. Prevailing winds are described by the direction from which they are blowing. A "westerly" wind, for example, comes from the west.

The "horse latitudes" were named by sailors years ago. If ships carrying horses got stuck in these windless areas and ran out of horse feed, they threw the animals overboard.

Seasonal Winds

Seasonal winds are winds that blow only at certain times of the year and only over one or two countries. In Asia, for example, monsoon winds–large-scale land and sea breezes–are produced by changes in pressure systems. In winter, dry sinking air forms a large, high-pressure area over the continent. Winter monsoon winds blow away from the coast so the weather is dry. In the summer, the land heats faster than the sea, weakening the high-pressure system and causing the winds to reverse direction. The summer monsoon brings moist air from over the sea into the dry continent and creates a sudden and dramatic change in the weather. Heavy, or even torrential rains, dump their moisture on the dry Earth. It is the presence of these monsoon winds that give Asia a rainy season and a dry season.

Local Winds

Local winds can last for a few weeks or just a few hours. In coastal areas, local winds are produced by the cooling of land and water, while the shape of the land causes distinctively local winds in inland regions. These local winds have their own names. Rising (daytime) and sinking (nighttime) air from mountain ranges or hills, for example, are referred to as *anabatic* and *katabatic* winds respectively.

Local Winds of the World

Winds that always happen at the same time or in the same place are given special names. Here are a few examples:

- **Bhoots** blow in India.
- **Brickfielders** are hot, dusty northeast summer winds that blow through southeastern Australia.
- **Chinooks** (named after the Native American word for *snow-eater*) are warm, dry, west winds that rush down the slopes of the Rocky Mountains in the western United States and Canada. These winds, which are caused by the warming of the air by compression as it sinks, cause sudden, dramatic increases in temperature. (Temperatures rise 20 to 40 degrees in just 15 minutes!)
- **Doldrums** is the name given to the calm, almost still air found near the equator where the north and south tade winds meet.
- **Elephantas** blow in India.
- **Fohn** winds are European chinooks.
- **Haboobs** are African (northern Sudan) winds that are strong enough to create sand storms. They occur when columns of air rise rapidly as they are heated by the sun. The rising air carries desert sand and dust with it.
- **Kwats** blow in China.
- **Mistrals** are cold, dry, northerly winds that blow off the Mediterranean coast of Spain and France and are funneled along the Rhone valley.
- **Simooms** blow in North Africa.
- **Williwaws** blow in Alaska.
- **Xlokks** blow in Malta.
- **Zondas** blow in Argentina.

Local Wind Mix 'n' Match

Match the local wind with the correct region.

mistral	China
fohn	Malta
chinook	Argentina
williwaw	India
zonda	Alaska
bhoot and elephanta	Equator
doldrums	Australia
haboob	Africa
xlokk	United States/Canada
brickfielder	Europe
kwat	Spain/France
simoom	Sudan

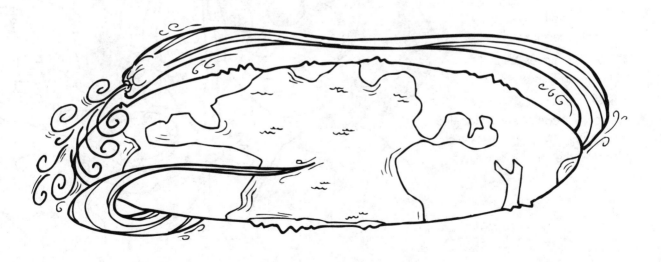

Wind Direction

Winds are often named according to the direction from which they come. A wind blowing in from the west, for example, is called a *westerly*, while a wind coming from the north is a *north wind*. Wind direction has a strong influence on weather. In North America, northerly winds usually mean cold weather. In North America and elsewhere, winds that blow in from across an ocean are more likely to bring rain than are those that have travelled across a mountain range or desert.

Wind direction is measured with a wind sock or an instrument called a *wind vane*. The simplest wind vane is shaped like an arrow with a very large, flat tail. The head of the arrow always points into the wind.

 ## Flag Flappers

A flag acts in much the same way as a wind vane. Make your own instrument to measure wind direction.

Materials

piece of cloth
stick
3 thumbtacks (or staples)
compass

What to Do

1 Attach the piece of cloth to the stick with the three thumbtacks.

2 Take your "flag" outside.

Questions to Ask

- Watch what happens.
- Does the cloth move when you hold the stick still?
- If the cloth moves, does it flutter just a little or stand straight out?
- Using your compass and looking at the flag, can you tell in which direction the wind is blowing?

108

Wind Speed

The instrument we use to measure wind speed is called an *anemometer*. The simplest type of anemometer was invented hundreds of years ago by Leonardo da Vinci. It measures the movement of a flat plate, mounted and facing into the wind.

Go Fly a Kite

Kites are more than just good fun on a windy day: they are a handy piece of equipment for measuring and observing the wind. With a kite, you can feel how strong the wind is and in which direction it is blowing. Kites are such good wind indicators, in fact, that in the 19th century-long before the invention of the airplane-meteorologists often used kites to record temperatures and measure wind speed high in the sky.

Acrostic Poems for Windy Weather

Write an acrostic poem to describe windy weather. As a class, brainstorm to come up with a list of words for each letter in, for example, the word *wind*. Then use these lists to help you create a rhyming poem in which the first letter of each line begins with a letter in the word *wind*. When you have created your class poem, have each student copy it and draw a picture to illustrate the poem.

W wet, wild, whip, whirl, water, wonderful
I icy, icky, inch, into, if, itchy, igloo
N noisy, nasty, nip, nibble, nod
D down, dreadful, drastic, drown

Wild, whipping, whirling wind
Icy at my back
Nipping at my nose and ears
Dragging down my pack.

Wind Gauge Whip-Up

You can make your own wind gauge. Although it will not give you an exact measurement of wind speed, it will give you a good indication of how quickly (and thus with how much force) the wind is blowing.

Materials

straight stick or broom handle
string
strip of toilet paper
piece of cardboard
pad of paper

What to Do

1 Tie the three objects side-by-side on the stick.

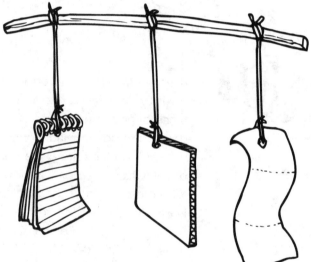

2 Take your wind gauge outside.

3 Have two students hold the stick between them, facing into the wind.

Questions to Ask

- What happens?
- Which material is the first to move?
- Which is the last?
- Keep your wind gauge in the classroom. Try taking it outside on different days. What happens in a light wind? What happens in a heavy wind?
- Keep track of your windy weather forecasts on this classroom chart.

	Day 1	Day 2	Day 3	Day 4	Day 5	Day 6	Day 7
pad of paper							
piece of cardboard							
strip of toilet paper							

The Beaufort Scale

The Beaufort scale is a wind-rating system named after Sir Francis Beaufort, the man who invented it. The Beaufort scale describes how the wind behaves at various speeds. See page 112 for illustrations.

Number	Description	Wind speed in km/h at 10 m above ground
0	Calm. Smoke rises vertically.	<1
1	Light air. Trees are still. Smoke drifts lazily. Wind does not move weather vanes.	1-5
2	Light breeze. Wind is felt on the face. Leaves rustle. Weather vanes move.	6-11
3	Gentle breeze. Leaves and twigs move. Flags flap.	12-19
4	Moderate breeze. wind lifts dust and leaves paper. Small branches move.	20-28
5	Fresh breeze. Small, leafy trees sway. Wavelets form on water.	29-38
6	Strong breeze. Large branches sway. Telephone wires hum. Umbrella blow around.	39-49
7	Near gale. Whole trees sway. Walking into the wind is difficult.	50-61
8	Gale. Twigs and branches snap off trees.	62-74
9	Strong gale. Slight damage to buildings. Roof tiles blow off.	75-88
10	Storm. Trees are uprooted. Buildings are damaged.	89-102
11	Widespread damage.	103-117
12	Hurricane. Very rare. Total destruction.	118+

In the spring of 1934, the winds at the peak of Mount Washington in the United States blew right off the top of the Beaufort Scale. They set a record measuring 231 mph (371 km/h). And just think, a wind that blows at 188 mph (303 km/h) can tear off your clothes!

The Beaufort Scale Wind Board Game

The object of the game is to have the wind blow your marker to the finish line but not blow you back! Winds up to six on the Beaufort scale move the player back the appropriate number of spaces; winds higher than six blow the player forward. Players draw Wind Cards to see how far and in what direction they are to move.

To begin:

1. Each player chooses a marker and places it on "START."
2. To decide who goes first, each player draws one Wind Card. Play begins with the player who draws the highest card. All cards are returned to the deck. Play continues clockwise.
3. Two players can occupy the same space at the same time.
4. It is not necessary to get the exact number to win.

   Note to teacher: Photocopy and cut out at least two of each of the Wind Cards below. Cards should be placed facedown in a pile. The gameboard should be enlarged on a photocopier.

Beaufort Scale Wind Board Game

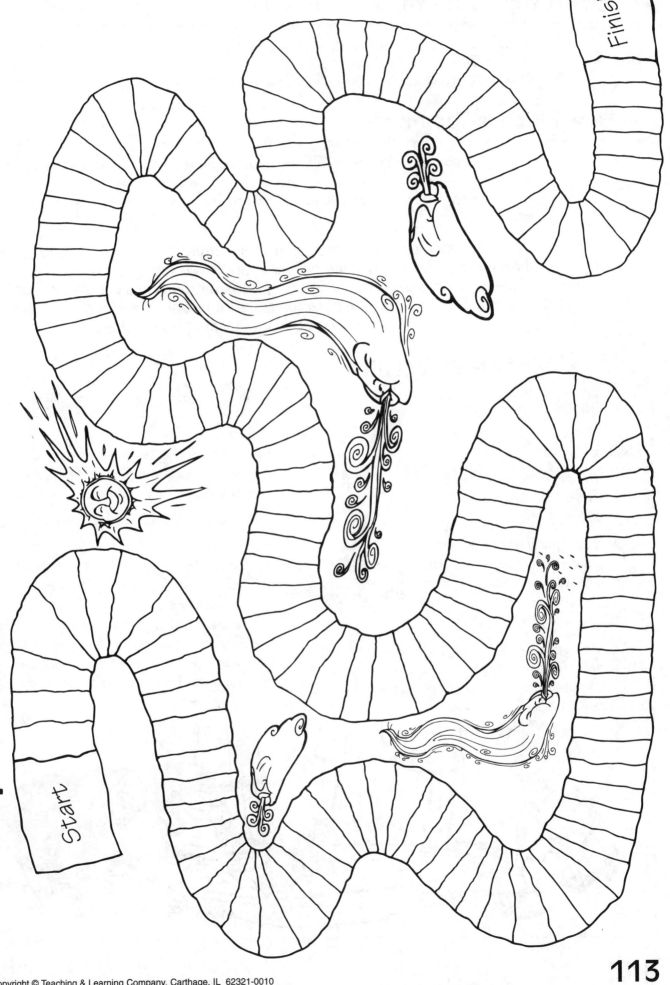

Finish

Start

Pick a Wind, Any Wind

If you could name your own wind, what would you call it?
How would it rate on the Beaufort Scale?
Can you describe what it would do to the things around you?

How Much Is Too Much?

Winds vary from gentle breezes to sudden, violent storms that can cause destruction and even death. A breeze on a hot, sunny day is a welcome relief – it makes us feel cool because it moves air over our skin. But the world's strongest winds are a nightmare – they can pick up cars and hurl them the length of a football field!

While thermometers tell us the actual temperature, the windchill measurement tells us how much colder it feels at various wind speeds. We feel colder when it is windy because the wind blows away the thin layer of warm air that usually surrounds our body and helps to keep us warm. Weather forecasters announce the windchill so that people will know how cold it will really feels out there.

Wind-at-Work Center

Set up a wind-at-work center.

1 Use straws to make wind to push paint around a piece of paper.

2 Make walnut boats. Place in a shallow pan. Have races with two children blowing on their boats to speed them to the other end of the "lake."

3 Mount pinwheels (see page 115) and create your own wind-generating station. See how much wind it takes to get all the pinwheels spinning . . . and stay spinning!

4 With teacher supervision, set up a clothesline. Dampen a few rags and pin to the line. Use a blow dryer to "air-dry" the laundry.

5 Creative Writing: "What Wind Does for Me"

6 **Wind Ball:** Place a Ping-Pong™ ball in the middle of a table. Use a piece of tape to make a goal line at each end of the table, about 4" (10 cm) from the edge. Divide students into teams. Have teams stand opposite one another across the table. At the word *go* teams blow, using their wind power to push the Ping-Pong ball™ across the opponent's goal line.

114

Wind at Work

Not all strong winds are destructive. They also do valuable work. They bring changes in the weather. They alter the face of the landscape. They carry pollen and seeds to new places. Trade winds push sailing ships across the ocean, and jet streams push planes across the sky. For centuries, windmills have harnessed wind power to drive machinery. Today, huge windmills or wind turbines-tall towers with large blades mounted on top-are used to generate electricity. They are placed in exposed, windy places, alone or in groups called *wind farms*. Although one large wind turbine can produce enough electricity to satisfy a small town, it takes many wind turbines to produce as much electricity as an ordinary power station. Wind turbines have the advantage of being "pollution free," but they are very noisy and require huge amounts of land.

The windiest place in the world is Commonwealth Bay in Antarctica, where gales commonly reach speeds of 200 mph.

Make a Pinwheel

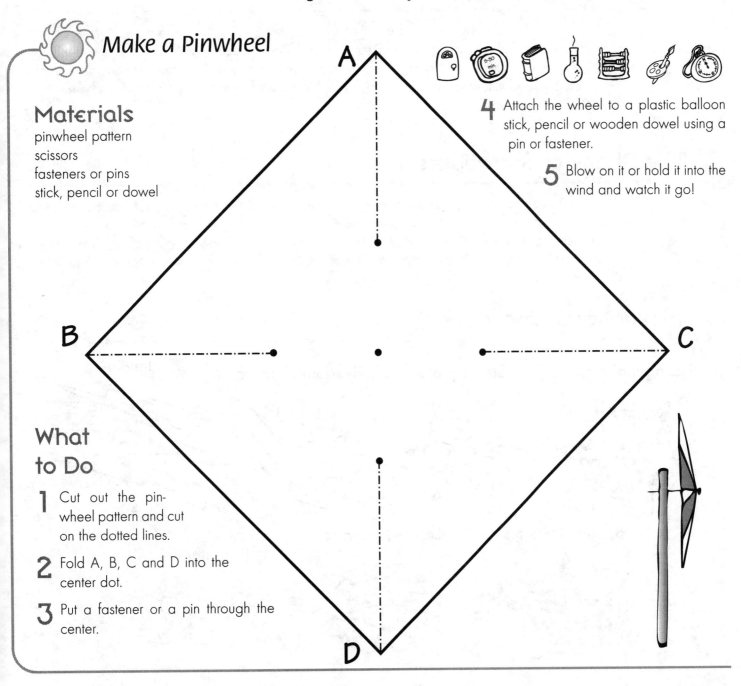

Materials
pinwheel pattern
scissors
fasteners or pins
stick, pencil or dowel

4 Attach the wheel to a plastic balloon stick, pencil or wooden dowel using a pin or fastener.

5 Blow on it or hold it into the wind and watch it go!

What to Do

1 Cut out the pinwheel pattern and cut on the dotted lines.

2 Fold A, B, C and D into the center dot.

3 Put a fastener or a pin through the center.

Chapter 8
Snow and Cold

The days are short and the nights are long. The water freezes over. The sun is low in the sky during the day; the thermometer has dipped very low. Bitter winds whip snow from the dark gray clouds and rattle the bare branches. We don our mittens, caps, parkas and snow boots and reach for our sleds, skates and snow shovels. It's winter!

The deepest covering of snow ever recorded was 37' 7" (1145.5 cm) in Tamarac, California, in March 1911.

What Is a Snowflake?

Two to six miles up in the sky, in a cloud that is colder that 32°F or 0°C, a droplet of water condenses around a speck of dust, bacteria or another ice crystal and freezes. As this ice crystal falls through the sky, its shape is affected by changes in air temperature, moisture and fluttering into another crystal. An ice crystal may fall for two hours and may travel hundreds of miles before floating to the ground with trillions of other snow crystals as a snowflake.

The Shape of Snowflakes

Snow crystals can be any number of shapes resembling everything from pencils to diamonds. Water molecules form together in a way that makes most snow crystals hexagonal or six-sided. Because of the way a snowflake is formed, it is almost impossible to find two snowflakes exactly the same, however, the many shapes can be categorized into the seven basic shapes of the International Snow Chart.

International Snow Chart

Hexagonal plate   **Stellar plate**   **Hexagonal column**   **Needles**

Spatial dendrites   **Capped columns**

Irregular crystals

Snow Types

Snowflakes occur in an infinite variety of shapes and no on has ever found two the same. All natural snowflakes are six-sided and consist of five crystals which are flat plates, rarer forms like needles and columns are sometimes found.

Three Basic Kinds of Snow

Dry, fluffy snow that floats from the sky. Usually star-shaped flakes from low, cold clouds.
Wet snow with crystals that resemble flat, six-sided discs and come from low, warm clouds.
Fine, dry, powdery snow is made of tiny crystals and blows around with a hissing sound. Comes from high, very cold clouds.

 Snowflakes

Materials
squares of paper–white or silver
scissors

What to Do

1 Fold the square of paper in half diagonally. Bring the two opposite corners together and fold.

2 Now bring the two opposite corners together and fold again.

3 Make zigzag or wavy cuts into the sides of the cone on the folded edges, but don't cut all the way across.

4 Unfold the paper and you have your very own original snowflake.

Freezing Temperatures: Too Cold to Snow?

If the air is very cold, not much snow can fall because cold air may not hold enough moisture for any kind of precipitation. The heaviest snowfalls occur in mild winter weather when the air holds the most moisture and the flakes are large. The colder the air, the finer the flakes become. Can it ever be too cold to snow? Well, no matter how cold the air is, it always contains some moisture. This moisture can fall in the form of tiny snow crystals as it sometimes does when it seems too cold to snow!

The lowest recorded temperature was -130°F (-63°C) at Snag, Yukon Territory, February 3, 1947.

Predict a Snowstorm

Use your barometer (page 40) to help you predict a snowstorm! Falling air pressure usually brings snow because air under low pressure rises and cools, making snow-filled clouds. When the air pressure increases, you're in for fine, dry wintry weather because air under high pressure sinks, making clear skies.

Snow Facts and Snow Folklore

There are about one million ice crystals in a patch of snow 2' (.61 m) wide, 2' (.61 m) long and 10" (25 cm) deep.

The greatest snowfall in one day (24 hours) was 78" (198cm). It fell at Mile 47 Camp, Cooper River Division, Arkansas, on February 7, 1963.

The greatest snowfall in one year: 1,224" –that's 102' (30.6 m)–at the Paradise Ranger Station, Mt. Rainier, Washington, between February 19, 1971, and February 18, 1972.

A university professor calculated that just one big snowstorm could drop 50 quadrillion snowflakes on his city.

Ten inches (25 cm) of freshly fallen snow is considered to be equivalent to 1" (2.5 cm) of rain (or 10 cm = 1 m). Melt some snow and find out if this is true. Results vary with the type of snow.

The odds of two ice crystals being exactly alike are estimated to be one in 105,000,000.

Some of the Earth's highest mountain peaks in the Himalayas near the equator are covered in ice and snow all year.

The heaviest snowfalls occur when the air temperature is hovering around freezing.

The snowiest part of the world is from about latitude 66 to latitude 40 in the Northern Hemisphere; all of the Canadian provinces, the southern parts of the Northwest Territory and the Yukon and about half of the United States are within these bounds.

If snow sticks to the trees, it won't stick around.

More snow falls in a year in southern Canada and the northern United States than at the North Pole.

Big, wet snowflakes are a sign of a short storm. The small, powdery dry flakes are a sign of a long storm.

When a dog howls at the moon in winter it is a sign of snow.

If snow begins in mid of day, expect a foot of it to lay.

Put a pint of snow from the season's first snowfall on a stove and slowly melt it. The number of bubbles that rise to the surface is the number of snowfalls to expect.

Study a Snowflake

Materials

square of black felt or cardboard
magnifying glass

What to Do

1 Put a square of black cardboard or felt outside away from the sunshine or in the freezer until it is cold.

2 Take the black squares outside on a snowy day and catch snowflakes.

3 Encourage students to observe and discuss the many snowflake patterns. Look at the snowflakes with a magnifying glass or a microscope. Compare the shapes of two flakes. How many different shapes can your students find?

4 Repeat this another day when the weather has changed. Are the flakes affected by the different weather conditions?

Try This

- Keep a notebook of your crystals. Record the air temperature on the day they are recorded. Make sketches of the crystals. Does air temperature affect the crystals?

The Snowflake Man

In 1880, at 15 years of age, Wilson Bentley came in contact with his first microscope. From that time on Bentley studied snowflakes under a microscope. For 48 years Bentley spent his winters in a cold, open shed catching snowflakes on a velvet-lined tray and quickly photographing them. He designed a method to take the first successful "photomicrograph" of an ice crystal. In his life he took over 5,000 photomicrographs, with almost half of them being published in 1931 in the still popular book, **Snow Crystals**. Bentley found that each snowflake was at least a little different from another.

Winter Storm Warnings

In the winter forecasters broadcast winter storm warnings, drifting snow and visibility, to help people prepare for the elements.

Blizzards

When heavy snowfall is accompanied by strong winds, it is called a *blizzard*. This combination of wind and snow may make it impossible to see, which makes travel and communication difficult. The wind piles huge drifts of snow against any obstacle and may completely cover cars and trains, trapping the passengers inside.

Blizzards can be very dangerous so weather forecasters announce weather warnings when they suspect one is approaching.

Blizzards leave a white trail of drifts and snowbanks that make it difficult to get your car out of the driveway but easy for you to build great snow forts!

Sculpt the Snow

Get creative and venture beyond the simple snowman.

Materials

snow (slushy snow works best especially on a warm day after a snowfall)

waterproof gloves

shaping, smoothing and carving tools: containers, sticks, shovels, kitchen utensils

coloring: 1 cup (240 ml) water and 8 drops food coloring in a spray bottle

decorations: cranberries, carrots, twigs, raisins, nuts, balls, stones or recycled materials

props: clothing, footwear, toys, sports equipment or flags

What to Do

1 Choose a snowy location.

2 Plan for a wide, sturdy base to the sculpture.

3 Roll a snowball along the ground and watch it get larger and larger. You can shape the snowball by alternating the side it is rolled on.

4 Stack, shape and combine various balls until you have a basic shape. It is best to begin with simple shapes like snowpeople, bunnies, whales, bears, cars, etc.

5 Smooth, carve and sculpt with carving tools.

6 Add details, color and decorations.

Try This

- Choose a theme and create a snowball farmyard (add straw, overalls, feathers, brown eggs), zoo or circus (give a human figure a clown nose, a seal with a ball, a zebra with black stripes) or dinosaurs (spray them green and make some giant dinosaur eggs).

- Host a Snow Show. Take photographs and admire your work.

Snowrollers

When the weather conditions are just right, you might see a giant snowball go by! Snowrollers, as these are called, occur in the open countryside when the snow is wet and the wind is strong. The wind rolls giant balls or doughnuts of snow across the open fields to create quite a spectacle!

Take a Closer Look

- Have you ever really looked at snow? It is a wonder to behold! Sharpen your observation skills by thinking about snow and taking a closer look.
- Look at it up close and from afar, feel it, smell it and record your findings.
- What happens when you pour water onto snow or ice?
- What changes do you see when you bring snow indoors? What happens when you take it back out? Use a thermometer to monitor temperature.
- Can you make snow stick together?
- Melt snow in a coffee filter. What do you see on the filter?
- Is there a difference between fresh snow and snow that is a few days old?

How Cold Is It?

Materials

thermometer

What to Do

1 Place your thermometer in a location out of the direct sunlight.

2 Observe the thermometer reading and record.

How Much Snow Has Fallen?

Make a depth gauge to find out how much snow has fallen today.

Materials

large, wide-mouthed plastic container
masking tape, about 6" (15 cm) long
measuring tape
permanent marker
open area
snowfall

What to Do

1 Stick a piece of masking tape on the outside of the jar. Mark it in $1/2$" (1.25 cm) intervals with a marker.

2 Place in an open environment, free from obstacles or obstructions.

3 Measure and record the measurements.

Try This

- Use an ordinary ruler to measure the newest layer of snowfall. When fresh snow has fallen on old snow, gently dig a hole until you can see a line dividing the two layers of snowfall.

Snow Cover

Snow, Snow, Melt Away

Heat moves warm to cold; from warm air to cold snow. When the ground is covered with snow, it may take the snow a long time to melt because it reflects most of the sunlight. If the surface melts on top and then refreezes, the snow cover will last even longer. A warm air mass is generally what it takes to melt away the snow.

How Deep Is It?

Make a depth gauge to find out how much snow has fallen so far this winter.

Materials

yard stick or meterstick

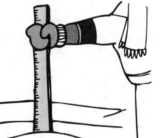

What to Do

1 Push the stick through the snow until you hit ground.

2 Take the reading from the measurement on the stick.

3 Make a few measurements and then take an average to compensate for drifting snow.

How Much Moisture?

Make a moisture indicator to determine the amount of moisture present in the atmosphere at a particular place and time.

Materials

tacks
wooden stake
8" (20 cm) piece of undeveloped photographic film

What to Do

1 Tack one end of the film to the top of the stake.

2 Mark 5 mm intervals on the stake.

3 Record the extent to which the film has curled or uncurled according to your scale.

How Cold Is the Snow?

Determine the temperature of snow at various depths.

Materials

3 thermometers
shovel
snow

What to Do

1 Dig a hole in the snow all the way to the ground or as deep as you can.

2 Place one thermometer in the snow closest to the ground, one half down your hole and one about one 1" (2.5 cm) the surface.

3 Let the thermometers sit for 15 minutes before taking temperature readings.

4 Compare the temperatures and try to account for these readings.

Name _____

Tracks in the Snow

Look for tracks in the snow and try to identify them using this sheet.

Dog

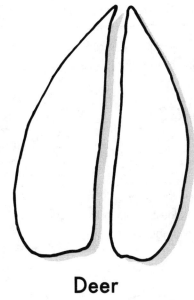

Deer

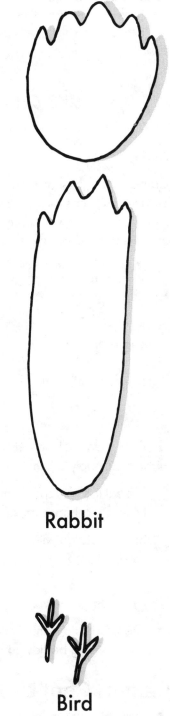

Rabbit

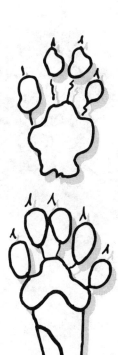

Mouse

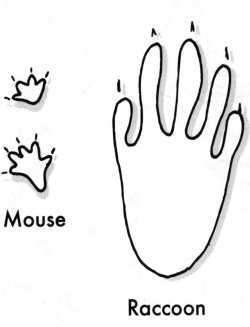

Raccoon

Bird

Squirrel

Ice

Something amazing happens to water when the temperature reaches the freezing point (32°F or 0°C). It becomes a solid and we call that solid water ice!

Icicle Watch

Observe an icicle dripping on a warm day. Hang one outside the classroom window where children can watch it carefully throughout the day.

Make an Ice Slide

Caution: A child should not go down the slide until the previous child has cleared away from the bottom of the slide. Do not allow children to stand at the top as they prepare to go down the slide.

Turn a slope into an exciting ice slide.

Materials

slope
freezing temperatures
snow
water spray (optional)

What to Do

1 Pack a path all the way down the hill using flat surfaces. Apply a light spray and let it freeze.

2 Repeat this light spray and freezing routine until you have a solid base on the slide.

3 Spray the slide with a good spray and let it freeze solid.

Try This

• Discuss friction and watch what happens when many sliding bodies go down the slope.

Design Challenge

• Ask students to design a better sled and make a model of it to try on the ice slide.

124

Ice Skating

Make a School Yard Skating Rink

Winter, water, a little work and a wonderful winter wonderland!

Materials

water
natural rubber hose
snowshoes or skis
snow shovel or scraper
12 to 14 hours of your time
optional: 1" x 6" (2.5 x 15 cm) lumber (new or reclaimed), 3" (8 cm) nails for the corners (or brackets and screws) and 2" x 4"s (5 x 10 cm) for strong backs to anchor the boards from the rear

What to Do

1 Plan the location and dimensions of your rink.

2 Pack the snow down in the designated area by wearing snowshoes, skis or big boots! Attempt to make the area as smooth and flat as possible.

3 Shape the surrounding snow to form banks. (Optional: Place 1" x 6"s [2.5 x 15 cm] around the border. Nail the corners with scrap wood nailed to the back side. Build up the snow to anchor the boards.)

4 Add the essential ingredient–water! Spray a light application of water and let it freeze. Repeat this process three or four times until you have a solid base.

5 Flood the ice heavily once the base is built up. Build up the low areas until you have a smooth uniform surface.

6 Maintain a bump-free surface with a light application of water once a week or so depending on the usage of the rink.

7 Clear the rink after snowfalls using a snow shovel.

Very cold temperatures will cause the water to freeze before it has had a chance to spread evenly.

Too much water can create a thin cavity. Break the thin layer on these cavities, and pack the hole with slushy snow and water.

Plan a Skate Exchange

Have your students' feet grown two sizes since last winter? Do you have some skateless children? Help students organize a skate exchange! Take this opportunity to raise funds for a classroom venture or to cover the costs of the outdoor rink, provide a lesson in sharing and recycling and teach your students math and business skills.

Skate Fitting and Care Tips

The Best Fit

- Properly fitting skates should allow two finger-widths between the child's heel and the heel of the skate.
- Good quality leather, lace-up skates, with good ankle support, sharpened and laced tightly are best.
- Dry blades off after skating to prevent rusting and remove skate guards when storing.
- Protect leather skates with a clear coat of wax.
- Sharpen skates when they get dull.

Tips for Tots

- Some children are natural skaters; others will need lots of practice.

- Beginning skaters should wear a helmet for protection and proper wear for falling and sliding on the ice.

- Help a child gain confidence balancing on those thin blades by enlisting the help of older students as partners or providing pile-pilons, small chairs or skating bars to be pushed around the ice by new skaters those first few times around the rink.

- Beginners should first master getting up off the ice. Skaters can hold their arms out to the side for balance and begin by walking on their skates, marching on their skates and then gliding.

- Stopping and turning on skates will follow as children gain experience.

126

Frost

Have you seen Jack Frost's work on a windowpane or on the branches of a tree?

When a cold, clear, dry night follows a cold winter's day, a sharp frost is likely to settle just about anywhere. The ground temperature drops more sharply at night when there are no clouds in the sky.

When dew forms on glass and is cooled to freezing point, it turns into patterns of ice crystals which transform windows into wintry masterpieces. The frost is white because of the air contained in the ice crystals. On especially cold evenings, watch for the delicate fern patterns on the inside of windows.

Hoar frost occurs when water vapor touches a very cold surface and freezes almost instantly, forming spiky needles of hoar frost on leaves and branches and metal surfaces. Hoar frost tends to occur when moist air reaches a temperature of about 32°F or 0°C and the ground is much colder.

 ## Frosty Patterns

Frost often covers the trees and ground in cold weather. See how frost forms.

Materials

cotton swab
petroleum jelly
spoon
glass
crushed ice
salt

What to Do

1 Smother your cotton swab in petroleum jelly.

2 Paint a simple pattern, design or shape on the outside of a glass with the jelly.

3 Fill the glass ³/₄ full with crushed ice.

4 Add salt and stir it all together.

5 Observe the glass for several minutes. A frost pattern will slowly form on the outside of the glass as water vapor in the air condenses on the cold surface of the glass and freezes to form a thin layer of ice crystals. Where there is greasy petroleum jelly, water can't condense on the glass and no frost will form.

Try This

• Breathe on a window on a cold day; then observe condensation or frost designs on the window.

Critter Care

Animals are very much affected by the weather. Some migrate, some hibernate and some survive. Animals have their own methods for surviving the winters. Some conserve energy, some hibernate, some snuggle together and some are provided with insulation in the form of a layer of fat, a thicker fur coat or extra feathers.

Try This

- Leave some treats for the winter birds and critters who are trying to survive in your area. Try to locate these in a position where you can observe the wildlife.

Snowmen? They're for the Birds

Decorate the snowman with birdseed, peanut butter seed balls, bread cubes, peanuts in their shells and berries.

Edible Strings

String some edibles. String cotton thread with cranberries or other red, edible berries; apple rings; kiwi fruit or oranges and hang from poles or branches.

Critter Cone

Spread peanut butter or suet on a pinecone, sprinkle it with birdseed and hang out for the birds.

Snow White Hot Chocolate

After playing in the snow or when celebrating a winter festival, there is nothing more satisfying than a steaming mug of hot chocolate. This recipe offers an aesthetically intriguing twist to an old favorite.

Materials

white chocolate baking squares (8 ounces [226.8 g])
4 cups (960 ml) of water
12 cups (2880 ml) of milk
large saucepan
whisk
mugs
mini marshmallows, white
    chocolate shavings or
    whipped cream

What to Do

1 With adult supervision, eat the white chocolate and water over medium heat. Stir constantly until melted.

2 Bring the mixture to a boil and then simmer for two minutes.

3 Add the milk and heat thoroughly, stirring occasionally.

4 Ladle into mugs, top with a fluffy white topping of marshmallows, shavings or whipped cream. (Serves 25 to 30 children.)

Questions to Ask

- Stir up some hot chocolate and talk about keeping warm. Discuss hypothermia, winter survival techniques and layering winter clothing.

- Talk about the history of winter wear: boots, zippers, fur coats, waterproof fabrics, ice skates and ski equipment.

Insulation from the Cold

The bodies of winter animals prepare them for winter survival by providing them with an insulating layer of fat, fur or feathers for warmth. You can insulate yourself from the cold by wearing layers of clothing that will trap air and keep you warm.

Air Insulation

A thin layer of air surrounding your body is heated by your body heat and acts like a layer of insulation to keep you warm. When the wind blows, you lose this warming layer.

 ## Don't Wait . . . Insulate!

Cold things gain heat when they melt and warm things can lose heat. Challenge children to slow these processes down by using different materials as insulators.

Materials

2 warm potatoes per child
foil wrap
vinyl
cotton cloth
wool cloth
snow and below freezing temperatures
timers (stopwatches, wristwatches, classroom clock)

What to Do

1 Challenge participants to make snow last indoors and keep hot potatoes hot outdoors.

2 Provide various insulating materials to assist with this challenge.

Try This

- Discuss winter clothing. Which materials are better insulators? Why does layering clothing keep you warm?

130

Snowball Math

Put children to work making math manipulatives out of snow!

Materials

snow
watch or stopwatch
snowball math chart
pen and clipboard
measuring tape/group

What to Do

1 Have students make snowballs, as many as they can in a five-minute time frame.

2 Start and stop the stopwatch announcing the start and stop times!

3 Have each group count the number of snowballs they made and record their answers on the Snowball Math worksheet on page 132.

4 Children should visit each group and talk about whether they made more or less snowballs and record their findings on the Snowball Math page.

5 Have children group snowballs according to size.

   a. Estimate and record the circumference of their largest snowball.

   b. Measure and record the actual circumference of the snowball.

   c. Record the difference between the estimated and actual size.

   d. Answer the questions on their chart.

Try This

- Encourage children to sort and discuss the various attributes of their snowballs. Provide a balance and weigh scale so children can weigh their snowballs.

Snowball Math

My group made _____ snowballs.

We made more snowballs than _____ groups and less snowballs than _____ groups.

I estimate the circumference of our largest snowball to be _____.

Our largest snowball has an actual circumference of _____.

The difference between our estimate and the actual circumference was _____.

If we added 5 more snowballs, we would have _____ snowballs.

If we took away 8 snowballs, we would have _____ snowballs.

If we multiplied our collection of snowballs by 2, we would have _____ snowballs.

132

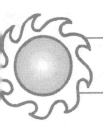

Chapter 9
Weather . . . in the Extreme

Most storms are the result of a collision of warm and cool air. When the two different types of air meet, the cold air forces the warm air upwards. Warm air is lighter and can hold more water vapor than cold air, but when it rises, it cools. After it cools, it cannot hold as much water vapor. The water vapor condenses into water droplets (or ice crystals) and a cloud is born. When the water vapor condenses, it releases heat. This heat helps to maintain the warmth of the air, which continues to rise until a towering storm cloud develops.

In temperate climates, warm and cold air masses meet or "converge" along an imaginary line called a *front*. When warm air moves towards cool air along a warm front, the warm air creeps up over the cool air. The result of this gentle movement is rain. If, however, cool air is moving along a cold front, it pushes the warm air up more aggressively and the results are more dramatic-thunderstorms, in many cases. While this lifting action is the cause of isolated storms, more violent storms-like hurricanes and tornadoes-occur ahead of cold fronts when winds converge over a broad area.

What Is Lightning?

Lightning is a giant electric charge that runs between thunderclouds or between a thundercloud and the ground.

In good weather, the ground surface is negatively charged, while high up in the sky (in the ionosphere) the air is positively charged. A slight current flows between the air and the ground, insulated by the rest of the air inbetween. However, all this changes on hot, humid days when thunderclouds develop and intensify the normal electrical field by more than 10 times.

Inside a thundercloud warm air rises rapidly, cools at the top of the cloud, starts to sink, warms as it sinks, then rises again. This turbulent motion causes the top of the cloud to become positively charged with electricity and the bottom of the cloud to become negatively charged. Although scientists are not exactly sure how this happens, they think it has something to do with the collision of small ice particles as they move around on strong air currents inside the thundercloud. These collisions create static electricity. The positively charged ice particles move up, accumulating at a high level, while negatively charged hailstones fall downwards and gather at the bottom of the cloud. The static electricity continues to build in the cloud until the difference between the positive and negative charges is large enough to overcome the insulation of the air. Then it sparks.

Lightning starts when energy sparks from the negatively charged cloud bottom to the positively charged ground. The negative downward energy charge of the "leader" carves out a hot pathway in the air. It is met by a positive upward flash from the ground (the "return stroke") moving along the same path. The flashes continue to travel up and down until the charge between cloud and ground has been "equalized" by the lightning. There are usually several up and down strokes in the same lightning bolt (one record breaker had 26!), but it all happens so fast-most lightning flashes last less than $1/5$ of a second!-that your brain thinks it has only seen one flash.

Thunder and Lightning

In ancient times, people believed that thunder was sound we heard when the gods were bowling or battling in the heavens. Today, however, we know this is not true. Thunder is the auditory part of the sound and light show we call thunder and lightning.

Static Electricity

The static electricity inside a thundercloud is the same kind of electricity you feel when you shuffle across a carpet in your stocking feet and then touch something. Of course the buildup of static electricity in a thundercloud is much bigger and has the potential to do a lot more damage.

Static electricity is defined as electricity that is at rest, or stationary electric charges.

The difference in electrical charge between the bottom of a thundercloud and the ground can be more than 305 volts per foot (1,000 V/m). A lightning spark releasing that kind of electrical potential has a tremendous amount of energy.

Static Cling

You can create your own static electricity. Blow up a balloon. Using a quick, back-and-forth motion, rub the balloon on your hair or clothes. Touch the balloon to your hair, clothes or a wall. What happens and why? (Much like the colliding action of the water droplets in a cloud, rubbing gave the balloon a positive charge. As a result, it "reaches out" and clings to negatively charged objects.)

Static electricity can be embarrassing! Have you ever been a victim of static cling?

Play It Safe

Because lightning takes the fastest route to Earth, it often strikes tall objects like buildings and trees. This tendency allows us to take certain precautions during an electrical storm.
Stay away from trees, open water and hilltops.

- Crouch or lay down in a low area.
- Remove metal jewelry and buckles.
- Stay away from open doors and windows.
- Do not use or stand near a telephone.
- And, of course, NEVER FLY A KITE!

*Many buildings are fitted with a thin metal pole called a **lightning rod**. The rod becomes a high point and a good target for lightning. If the rod is struck, and this is the intention, it leads the lightning safely to the ground.*

Likely Lightning Strikes

In the picture below, draw lightning between the clouds and the objects and areas it is likely to strike.

Flash in a Pan

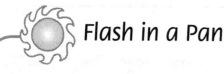

The strong positive electrical charge at the top of a thundercloud and the equally strong negative charge at the bottom are "insulated" by the air inbetween. Because the two conducting bodies are separated (insulated) from one another, no current runs between them and the electrical charges are "static." Only when the static electricity builds to the point where it can overcome the insulation of the air, does current flow between the two, creating lightning. Static electrical charges are all around us. Make your own electrical charges.

Materials

rubber glove
dish towel
screwdriver
metal baking pan

What to Do

1 Put the glove on your hand. (It will insulate you from any electrical current that is created.)

2 Using your gloved hand, rub the pan lightly on the dish towel for several minutes. (This will build up a static electrical charge.)

3 Turn off the lights.

4 Slowly bring the metal tip of the screwdriver close to (but not touching) the bottom of the pan.

"Lightning" will jump between the bottom of the pan and the tip of the screwdriver. You might even hear the crackling sound of "thunder."

Try This

- Rub two articles of clothing together for several minutes. When they "cling" together, turn off the lights and pull them apart. The sparks will fly!

- Choose a partner. Shuffle around on the carpet in your stocking feet, careful not to touch anything. Move towards your partner with your index finger extended. As your fingertips come close together, a spark of "lightning" will arc between them.

LifeSaver® Lightning

Materials

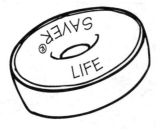

wintergreen-flavored LifeSavers®
mirror

What to Do

1 Stand in front of a mirror in a dark room.

2 Pop a few LifeSavers® into your mouth.

3 Chew them with your mouth open.

As your teeth crush the LifeSavers®, the sugar crystals in the candy are pulled apart and give the chunks of candy an electrical charge. Some pieces of candy will carry a positive charge, others will carry negative charge. Sparks of electricity leap between the pieces, made visible by the wintergreen oil.

Lightning Maze

Find the path through this lightning maze.

Start

Finish

The Different Faces of Lightning

Not all lightning is the same. Although lightning does flash between a cloud and the ground, this is only one direction the spark can take. More often, lightning flashes inside a cloud or between two clouds, and never actually reaches the ground.

Sheet lightning is the reflection of a lightning flash hidden by clouds. It looks like a white flash that lights up the whole sky.

Forked lightning occurs when energy travels from a cloud down to the ground following the easiest route ("the path of least resistance"). Because this path is usually irregular, the flash is forked or jagged. The first flash "ionizes" the air giving it an electrical charge which makes a path for the much brighter return flash.

What Is Thunder?

The electrically charged particles that make up a flash of lightning travel at the speed of light. They also carry heat. As they pass through the air they make it hot—five times hotter than the surface temperature of the sun! Fortunately, this extreme heat lasts only a few millionths of a second, but during that short time, it causes the air to expand violently. Thunder is the sound we hear as the heated air collapses—or explodes—as it cools. The sudden expansion of air, followed by its rush back into the partial vacuum that has been created, sends shock waves in all directions. It is those shock waves—the sound of the explosion—that is audible as thunder. Because light travels faster than sound, we see the lightning before we hear the thunder.

Thunder Forecasting: Near or Far?

Sharp cracks of thunder mean that lightning is nearby. Low, rumbly thunder usually means it is farther away. You can tell the distance between you and a storm by counting the seconds between a flash of lightning and the clap of thunder. There is a five-second pause between lightning and thunder for every mile of distance (three seconds for every kilometer). If the two happen at almost the same time, a flash and then a sharp CRACK, the storm is directly overhead!

Questions to Ask:

If you count 20 seconds between a flash of lightning and a clap of thunder, how far away is the storm? (Answer: 4 miles. $20 \div 5 = 4$).

Thunder in a Can

You can make your own thunder using an unopened can of soda.

The air inside a soda can is held under pressure. When you open the can, you release the pressure. The air expands, rushing in to fill the vacuum in the can. The "pfzzzzzzzz" that you hear when the can is opened is the sound made by the air as it expands and rushes into the vacuum. This "thunder" is the same sound that is made by air when it is heated by lightning, expands and then quickly cools. The faster the air expands, the louder the sound.

Try This

- Make paper thunder by filling a paper bag with air. Twist the mouth of the bag to trap the air inside. Pop the bag by striking it with your free hand.
- Use an inflated balloon and a pin or stomp on an empty, refolded cardboard milk carton.

138

Imagine a Storm

To make the concept of a thunderstorm more real, try a visualization or guided imagery exercise.

Have students spread out and sit comfortably on the floor. Ask them to close their eyes and listen to the story you are going to describe, doing their best to visualize a summer storm by conjuring up pictures in their minds. As you describe a series of images, make sure you leave some time between phrases for students to visualize the images you are suggesting. Before beginning, ask the students to be one of the following: themselves, a wild animal, a domestic animal . . .

It is summer . . . The air is hot and heavy with moisture . . . You hear the sounds of summer (heat bugs, birds singing, children laughing) . . . Suddenly, you become aware of a change in the weather: a coolness, a rustling of leaves in the trees . . . The sky turns dark, and menacing . . . In the distance, a bright flash of lightning splits the sky . . . After a long wait, you hear the rolling, rumbling sound of thunder . . . The lightning moves closer, the rumbles grow louder . . . Suddenly, lightning flashes and lights up the sky . . . A loud CRACK of thunder follows almost immediately . . . The wind is blowing almost savagely . . . The storm is overhead . . . You need to find shelter, a safe place to wait out the storm . . . Lightning flashes all around you . . . The sound of the thunder is deafening . . . The BOOMs are so loud and so frequent the Earth seems to shake . . . There are no longer times of quiet between the lightning and the thunder . . . You are afraid.

And then, suddenly, startlingly, it becomes still . . . Lightning flashes again, but in the distance . . . Far away, thunder rumbles . . . You come out of hiding . . . There is a new smell in the air, a freshness, a crispness . . . You can feel it on your skin, taste it in your mouth . . . You become aware of a new sound, a "ssshhhhhhhhh"ing sound . . . It is growing louder . . . You are not sure about the sound, but somehow you know you need to find shelter again . . . A new place, a dry place . . . And then, the air is filled with rain . . . It falls in a sheet, there are no spaces between raindrops . . . The rain has a loud, rich, constant sound . . . It rains and rains . . . The hard, dry ground runs with rivers of mud . . . And still the rain pounds down . . . Will it ever stop?

Yes. As suddenly as it began, the rain is gone . . . There is a stillness in the air, broken only by the soft dripping of water from leaves and eaves . . . The storm has passed . . . Once again, you come out of hiding, and a single bird begins to sing.

Wait a few seconds and then tell the students to open their eyes. What did they see and feel during the imaginary storm? Were they wild or domestic animals, or themselves? What shelter did they find and where? And what happened to them as the storm came and went?

After the students have shared their descriptions, discuss the idea that at one time or another, all creatures – great and small, everywhere in the world – will experience the kind of anxiety and need that you just experienced. Remind students that the next time they see lightning, hear thunder and feel the rain to think for a moment about the other creatures that might be feeling the storm.

Try This

- Have students draw pictures of what they imagined at each stage of the storm.

- Have students write a story about what they saw, heard, felt and did during the storm.

- Put on mini plays, acting out the part of each group – wild and domestic animals and people.

Thunderstorm Watch

The rumble of thunder is often the first indicator that an electrical storm is on its way. When you hear this sound, pay close attention to changing weather conditions and get ready for the worst.

Set up a classroom thunderstorm watch.

What to Do

Listen for the distant rumble of thunder. Then watch the sky for lightning. If both lightning and thunder are present, count the seconds to find out how much time elapses between the lightning flash and the thunderclap. Record the amount of time. Using the "five seconds/mile" equation (see page 138) figure out how much distance is between you and the storm. Continue to time the lightning/thunder interval. Is the storm moving towards you or away from you? How fast is the storm moving?

Lightning Does Strike Twice

Although it is commonly believed and said that "lightning never strikes twice," it does!

- Roy "Dooms" Sullivan, of Virginia, has been hit by lightning seven times.
- The CN Tower, in Toronto, Canada–the world's tallest, free-standing structure–is struck by lightning about 65 times each year.

Lightning Facts

Did you know that . . .

- there are about 2,000 thunderstorms raging in the world right this minute, and in the time it has taken you to read this sentence, lightning has struck about 500 times?
- there are 100 lightning flashes every second of every day?
- a single bolt of lightning contains enough electricity to power an average home for two weeks?
- a lightning bolt can be as long as several miles but no thicker than a finger?
- few lightning strikes cause damage?
- you have a one in 1.7 million chance of being struck by lightning?
- approximately 100 Americans (15 Canadians) are killed every year by lightning?

In one year, a town in Indonesia once experienced thunderstorms on 322 different days!
That is almost 11 months worth of thunderstorms!

What Is Wrong with This Picture?

Circle the things that the people in this picture should not be doing during a thunderstorm. Color the picture.

Hurricanes

The biggest and most powerful storms known to humankind are called *hurricanes*. They are circular and vary in size, but diameters of 400 miles (650 km) and wind speeds of 125 mph (200 km/h) are not uncommon. Hurricanes can last up to 10 days before they become regular rain-bearing storms, and at their height release as much energy as a hydrogen bomb every minute.

Hurricane Gilbert, which struck in 1988, was 930 miles (1,500 km) across!

Hurricanes start out as ordinary tropical storms over oceans that have surface temperatures of more than 80°F (27°C). When the water is that warm, it evaporates. The air becomes warm and humid and rises, creating an area of low pressure. If the surrounding air is already disturbed–by rain or showers, for example–it may rush in to replace the rising air, causing winds to come together and blow upward. Differences in air pressure cause the winds to swirl around each other as the doughnut-shaped storm gains strength. If the wind speed of the tropical storm reaches 74 mph (120 km/h) or more, the storm is "upgraded" to a hurricane.

One of the first signs of a hurricane is thick cirrus clouds.
Light rain soon becomes torrential, driven by a wind that grows rapidly stronger.

Once formed, hurricanes follow a path that leads away from the equator. They travel great distances, growing in intensity as long as they stay over warm water and are fuelled by rising water vapor. Once a hurricane moves over cool water or land, however, the fuel source is lost and the storm begins to die down.

Over the years hurricanes have caused unbelievable damage, sinking ships, destroying homes, ravaging crops and claiming the lives of millions of people and animals. Today, the Atlantic Ocean gives rise to about six hurricanes every year! Although we cannot lessen the severity of these storms, satellites and modern technology do allow weather experts to warn people of the approach of violent storms, giving them time to escape.

In 1881, 300,000 people were killed in Haiphong, Vietnam, by a typhoon.
In 1970, 500,000 people were killed in Bangladesh by a typhoon and the flooding it caused.

The Eye of the Storm

Air pressure in a hurricane is very low at the Earth's surface and high at the top of the storm. Warm, moist air, moving to the area of low pressure, rises and forms bands of up to 200 clouds in a vortex of fierce winds. At the center of this spiralling pinwheel of wind and cloud is a calm, cloudless center called the "eye." The strongest winds in a hurricane are the ones whirling around the eye in the "eye wall." These winds can reach speeds of up to 200 mph (320 km/h)–faster than a speeding train! The eye wall is created when a ring of warm, humid air rises from the sea. When it cools, some of it falls inward and sinks down slowly through the center of the storm.

The eye is the embodiment of absolute calm: no winds, no rain, just clear blue sky. It can sprawl up to 25 miles (40 km) across, and is often so wide that people are fooled into thinking that the storm has passed. They come out of hiding only to be smashed and pummelled by the opposite eye wall.

Great Walls of Water

The edges of a hurricane are relatively weak, but as the storm moves overhead, the winds travel faster than cars on the highway. These winds are so strong they can tear huge trees out of the ground by their roots, rip the roofs off houses and cause giant tidal waves and incredible flooding. In fact, much of the damage caused by hurricanes is due to water. Rainfall is heavy and winds produce waves up to 50 feet (15 m) high. This "tidal wave" effect is widespread, and even 9,000 miles (1,500 km) from the eye of the storm, waves are often much larger than normal. The fierce, pounding waves that travel in advance of a hurricane can reach 10' (3 m) in height.

A hurricane can drop as much as 10" (2.5 cm) of rain in just one day.

Model Hurricane

The clouds around a hurricane form spiral bands. In them, water vapor condenses in the warm, rising air. At high altitude the air enters the region of high pressure, adding to the pressure difference between the top and bottom of the storm. Some of the energy in the cloud is then transferred to the clear air next to each spiral band and increases the wind speed. Like air, spiralling water also forms bands.

Materials

squeeze bottle of food coloring (or eyedropper and coloring)
spoon
large glass bowl
water

What to Do

1 Fill the bowl with warm water.

2 Stir the water gently until it is moving in a slow circle around the bowl.

3 Squeeze a few drops of food coloring into the center of the bowl.

The color moves out and forms bands–just as clouds in a hurricane do.

143

Ancient Beginnings

The word *hurricane* comes from the Mayan word *Hunraken*, or storm god. In the Philippines hurricanes are known as *baguios*; in Australia they are referred to as *cyclones* and in China and Japan they are called *typhoons*. The word for *typhoon* is very similar in several eastern languages:

- In China, a violent rainstorm is a *ty-fong* meaning great wind.
- A whirlwind is known as a *tyfoon* in Arabic.
- The Polynesian storm god is called *Taafuna*.

Hurricanes, typhoons and cyclones are the same kind of storm. The only difference is that hurricanes arise over the Atlantic Ocean, typhoons are born over the North Pacific and cyclones begin over the Indian Ocean.

What's in a Name?

A hurricane, that's what! To tell different hurricanes apart, meteorologists have been giving them people names since 1953. Each year, meteorologists begin at the letter *A* and work their way through the alphabet, alternating between male and female names. To be fair, if one year starts with a boy, the next year starts with a girl. (This "equality" system was introduced in 1979–before that, hurricanes were only named after girls!)

Meteorologists never use the same name twice and, because they are too rare, they never use names beginning with the letters *Q, U, X, Y* or *Z*. Each year, the list of names is chosen in advance and so far, meteorologists have never reached the end of their list before they reach the end of the year.

The tradition of naming hurricanes apparently began when an American radio operator was whistling "Every Little Breeze Seems to Whisper Louise" during the broadcast of a storm warning. The storm was immediately christened Louise, and the tradition has continued ever since.

Hurricane Alphabet Math

It is possible to figure out how many hurricanes have already occurred at any given time of the year by finding out the name of the most recent storm and then counting back to *A*.

If Hurricane Douglas is battering the Florida Coast, how many hurricanes have there been this year?

Could there be a Hurricane Edward in the same year?

How many hurricanes will there have been when Hurricane Maureen strikes?

For more information on hurricanes, write to the National Hurricane Center, 1320 South Dixie Highway, Coral Gables, FL 33146.

Tornadoes

Tornadoes are the most violent of all wind storms. Much smaller than hurricanes, their winds are even more powerful. One tiny part of a spinning thunderstorm, tornadoes are sometimes no wider than a house, but they can pick up cows, rip the bark off trees, cause buildings to explode and send cars flying through the air.

Even though each tornado is only a few hundred meters in diameter, they contain enough energy to light up the streets of New York City for one whole night. The air inside a tornado storm cloud speeds upwards at as much as 100 mph (165 km/h).

Land-Born Demons

Fortunately, conditions have to be just right for a tornado to form. Unlike hurricanes, which begin over an ocean, the worst tornadoes form over land. Although tornadoes are fairly common the world over, three quarters of the world's worst tornadoes are born in the central United States in an area known as "Tornado Alley"–a chunk of land that covers nine states and runs from northern Texas through Oklahoma, Kansas and up into southern Iowa.

A tornado forms when cool, dry air moves in on hot humid weather. The warm air rises rapidly and is replaced by more warm air. Winds catch this rising air, spinning it over and over and then tipping it up on end. In this kind of spinning storm, warm, dry air sometimes blows into the middle of the cloud. There it cools and sinks quickly, drawing the spinning tunnel of winds down to the ground.

Do the Twist

Tornadoes, or "twisters" as they are sometimes called, zigzag across the country at speeds of up to 300 mph–the fastest winds known at ground level–destroying everything in their path. They are clearly visible to the naked eye because very low pressure in the whirling tunnel, or vortex, causes water vapor to condense, like rain in a rain cloud.

From a distance, tornadoes look like huge, dark elephants. The dark, moist thundercloud at the top of the tornado is filled with dust, water and small objects that have been whisked to the top of the funnel by incredibly strong winds. This upper cloud is named after the brass instrument it resembles–a tuba. The whirling, trunk-like funnel that reaches down from this cloud to the ground is like a giant vacuum cleaner hose: it sucks up everything it runs across, from chickens to cars!

Although some tornadoes are fairly short, others can be as long–or tall–as 1,000' (300 m). And, they can be anywhere from a few feet across to two miles (3.2 km) wide.

Like other winds, tornadoes are rated. The rating scale runs from F0 to F5. An F3 tornado travels around 125 mph (200 km/h). An F5 tornado can send a car flying the length of a football field!

Tornado in a Jar

A tornado is a *vortex* that begins high up in the air and reaches a funnel – a tube of fast, spiralling winds swirling around a calm center – down to the ground. Any liquid that turns quickly, such as water going down the drain, will form a simple vortex. Make your own vortex.

Materials

food coloring
spoon
tall glass jar
water

What to Do

1 Fill the jar almost to the top with cold water.

2 Stir the water with the spoon, keeping the spoon near the top of the water.

3 Make the water spin as fast as you can.

4 When the vortex appears, add a few drops of food coloring to the water. (This will make the shape of the vortex more visible.)

Try This

- Fill a jar with water. Add 1 teaspoon (5 ml) of salt and a very small drop of dish soap. Put the lid on the jar and tighten. Turn the jar on its side so it is horizontal to the ground and you are holding the lid in one hand and the bottom of the jar in the other. Swirl the water in the jar vigorously for several seconds.

It's Raining Cats and Dogs!

Tornadoes can lift almost anything, carrying its helpless victims for miles before the storm weakens and drops them again. Then small animals, and even cows, fall from the sky like rain.

Sometimes when a tornado is going over water, the funnel sucks up a mass of swirling water. The fish are kept aloft in the updraft until much later when the clouds disperse. Eventually rain falls, sometimes over land, and so do the fish!

146

Tornado Facts

Did you know that . . .

- most tornadoes travel at about 30 to 45 mph (50 to 70 km/h) - fast enough to tear roofs off houses and throw cars into basements?
- when a tornado passes over a building, the difference in air pressure can make the building explode?
- the best time to spot a tornado is between three in the afternoon and dinnertime?
- tornadoes kill more than 200 people each year in the United States alone?
- one day in 1974, 148 tornadoes swept through 13 states killing 315 people and causing $600 million in damage?
- tornadoes that form over water are called waterspouts and are less violent than tornadoes that form over land?
- there are other harmless funnels of air ("dust devils" or "whilly-whillies" often form in the desert without any sign of a storm and "snow devils" can spin up a flurry of snow and then disappear seconds later)?

We've Got a Lot to Learn

Because tornadoes are so difficult to observe - they are too violent, too small and too fast to study! - scientists still have a lot to learn about them. To find out exactly what is known, write to the National Severe Storms Forecast Center, Room 1728, 601 East 12th Street, Kansas City, MO 64106.

Hail

Hailstones are chunks of ice that grow inside thunderclouds and then fall from the sky. They can be as small as a pea or as big as a grapefruit.

Hailstones start out the same as many raindrops, as tiny crystals of ice in the upper part of clouds. Like raindrops, water droplets stick to these crystals and when they become heavy enough, they begin to fall through the cloud. Because the cloud is below freezing, the moisture in the cloud freezes into ice. Small hailstones are the ones that fall straight to the ground. Larger hailstones are formed when the frozen raindrop becomes trapped in the cloud and is thrown up and down by strong air currents. Each trip in this "elevator" causes yet another layer of water to stick to the hailstone and freeze. The size of the hailstone depends on how long it has been trapped in the cloud. Eventually, all hailstones become so heavy that they plummet from the cloud, or if the winds are really strong, they shoot up and out of the cloud like popcorn from a popper!

The Same but Different

Not all hailstones have the same shape. They can be round, flat or conical, but they are all made of layers of ice. If you took a hailstone and cut it open, you would see a series of rings inside. These rings are the different layers of the hailstone.

Although it doesn't seem very scientific, hailstones are measured according to their size:

- pea
- mothball
- marble
- Ping-Pong™ ball
- goose egg
- tennis ball
- melon

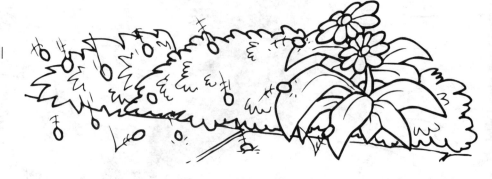

Hailing Humans

In 1930 during the Second World War, five German glider pilots became human hailstones. As their glider drifted through a thunderstorm they tried to parachute to safety. Instead, they were carried through the clouds on powerful thermal updrafts. Trapped in the clouds, they were tossed up and down again and again, getting coated with layer after layer of ice. Although the pilots eventually fell to Earth as human hailstones, only one of the five survived to tell the tale.

148

Make Your Own Hailstone

With a little wet snow and water and a lot of cold, you can make your own hailstone.

Materials

wet snow
spritzer bottle filled with water
freezer

What to Do

1 Take some wet snow and make a tightly packed, golf ball-sized snowball.

2 Put the snowball in the freezer.

3 When snowball is frozen, spray it with water and then put it back in the freezer.

4 Keep spraying and freezing the "hailstone" over the course of the next few days.

5 Then saw through the hailstone and look at the different layers.

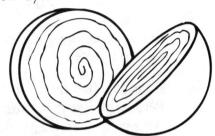

Hail Facts

Did you know that . . .

- in 1983, thousands of cattle were killed in Russia by huge chunks of falling ice?
- in 1983, 81 people were killed in China by hailstones weighing almost seven pounds (3 kg)?

Floods and Droughts

Most floods are caused by heavy rain. Water surges up from the sea battering coastlines and inland rivers swell and overflow their banks. When excess water flows across land, it travels at great speeds and depths, washing away bridges and homes, and claiming the lives of both animals and people. Flooding is most severe in low-lying places like Brazil, in South America, which is often hit by tropical storms and American states that are prone to hurricanes. Property damage as a result of a flood is often in the hundreds of millions of dollars.

Droughts occur when there is much less rain than usual in a particular area, or in areas such as East Africa that suffer from a persistent and **chronic** lack of rain. When water supplies run low or dwindle altogether, plants cannot grow and people and animals may die. Even deep underground water stores that exist below the surface of the Earth dry out after a drought and can take years to refill. Topsoil, the fertile top layer of soil in which plants grow, turns to dust and blows away making future agriculture difficult.

El Nino is the Christmastime warming of the ocean's surface off the coast of Ecuador and Peru. This warming starts a bizarre chain reaction in the atmosphere. El Nino has been known to turn the world's weather topsy-turvy drenching places that are normally dry and causing droughts in other countries during their rainy seasons.

Extreme Weather Word Association

Have children call out words they associate with extreme weather. Write these words on the chalkboard. Have the children make up a story or a poem using a selection of these words.

Extreme Weather Shape Stories

Using a pencil, lightly outline the shape of something that is associated with extreme weather. A lightning bolt or a tornado are good examples. Then write a story about the type of weather your shape represents. Write the words of the story along the outline of your weather indicator. Then erase the pencil outline.

Weather Word Search

Find each of the words listed at the bottom and circle in the puzzle. They can be found up, down, backwards and diagonally.

```
R  O  U  N  L  E  N  N  U  F  C  H
D  A  M  A  G  E  K  R  A  P  S  T
N  E  P  O  S  I  T  I  V  E  R  W
S  W  I  R  L  C  H  A  R  G  E  E
P  S  F  C  L  O  U  D  E  T  T  R
E  T  H  U  N  D  E  R  R  C  S  U
V  A  A  U  U  A  T  Y  F  C  I  S
I  T  I  B  R  N  P  L  E  M  W  S
T  I  L  H  D  R  O  U  G  H  T  E
A  C  H  T  H  O  I  H  R  D  O  R
G  W  I  N  D  T  H  C  I  A  D  P
E  E  N  O  L  C  Y  C  A  C  I  P
N  I  L  I  G  H  T  N  I  N  G  N
Y  T  I  C  I  R  T  C  E  L  E  Y
```

thunder	swirl	pressure	strike	rain
positive	eye	tornado	charge	ice
rod	drought	funnel	cloud	damage
air	lightning	wind	static	wet
electricity	negative	hail	twister	dry
cyclone	spark	flood	hurricane	

Chapter 10
Pollution and Our Changing Weather

Changing the Weather

Since early times people have wanted to have some control over the weather. There have been prayers, ceremonies, rituals and special dances thought to bring on the rains in times of drought, stop the rains in times of flooding, cause the snow to retreat for spring planting and so on.

In 1946 scientists discovered a process called cloud seeding. Tiny particles dropped into certain clouds could cause these clouds to release their rain. A similar method has been experimented with for alleviating fog at airports, reducing lightning and reducing the size of damaging hailstones.

Earth is a wonderful place that millions of living creatures call home. Every living thing from the smallest creature swimming in the sea to the largest elephant roaming the African plains, is important to the balance of life on Earth. Unfortunately, from the rain forests to the coral reefs, the life-style of humans is destroying the Earth's natural habitats to such a degree that many plants, animals and natural habitats can no longer survive.

The environments we construct affect the immediate weather of our communities. Our big cities are primarily built of materials that interrupt the water cycle. These building materials repel water causing rains to drain away to underground pipes before the water can evaporate and condense as a cloud. These concrete jungles warm the air, restrict the quantity of plant life which can return water to the air; cause the sun's energy to heat streets, sidewalks and buildings instead of evaporating water; and slow the wind, all of which interfere with the water cycle and warm the air.

Some aspects of our life-style have a harmful effect on our long-term weather patterns. Today many people live a life of luxury–a life that is changing our weather and hurting our planet. You might not notice it in your daily life, but the weather is changing, very slightly. Scientists believe that our life-style is affecting the balance of gases in the atmosphere, causing overall weather patterns to change at an unnatural rate. People are becoming more and more worried about the effect our pollutants are having on the health of our planet.

Pollution affects our weather and our planet in several ways.

Air Pollution

When air contains material that can cause harm or discomfort to living things or damage to property, it is called dirty or polluted air. Air pollution comes from vehicle exhausts, factories, furnaces and other sources and adds harmful gases to the troposphere each year. The weather on Earth is affected by pollution, especially air pollution.

Smokey-Fog

In 1905 Harold de Veaux called the smoke and fog of London, smog. Smog as we know it today consists of chemicals heated by the sun. All smogs are unpleasant and some are even dangerous.

 ## Make Your Own Smog

Materials

jar
water
aluminum foil
ice cubes
spoonful of salt
4" x 1" (10 x 2.5 cm) strip of paper twisted to make "firewood"
match (Adult use only!)

What to Do

1 Swish water around in the jar and pour it out.

2 Fit the foil over the jar and shape to fit the jar.

3 Remove the foil lid and put ice cubes on top of it.

4 Sprinkle salt over the ice cubes.

5 Have an adult light the paper on fire and place it in jar.

6 Quickly cover the jar with the foil lid and salted ice cubes.

Try This

• Research the Killer Smog that covered London in 1952. Five days of thick smog left 4,000 people dead!

Many countries are trying to clean up their air with various methods and laws such as the Clean Air Act.

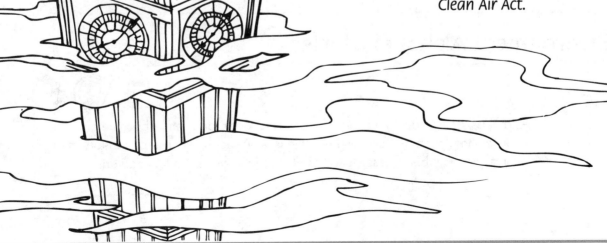

Air Pollution Indicator

Find out how much particulate matter there is in the air you breathe!

Materials

sturdy paper plates
microscope slides (optional)
scrap wood (a stick will work)
nail and jaw clip or tape
petroleum jelly

What to Do

1 Have students design a method for attaching a jaw clip to the end of a flat stick, using the materials above.

2 Thinly smear petroleum jelly on the slides or paper plates and attach to the stick. (In a highly contaminated area you will not need the microscope to help you see the particulate matter.)

3 Place the pollution indicator in a protected location where you want to test the air.

4 Place one test plate in the classroom as a control.

5 Observe your plates after several hours, a day and then a week.

6 Record your results by pasting them on a chart for all to see. Have students record their descriptions and reactions under the correct column.

Try This

- Discuss differences between natural particulate matter in the air and pollutants that can be harmful to our environment and health.

- Write a class letter to a business in your community which contributes to air pollution. Ask them about their plans for reducing pollution.

Environment Alphabet Stories

As a class, or individually, have students write a story (or poem) about the environment using the 26 letters of the alphabet. Beginning with the letter A, each new line of the story must begin with the next letter of the alphabet. These stories can be as long or as short as desired.

Global Warming

Most scientists believe that our activities are changing the atmosphere so much that the temperature of the Earth is rising, little by little. Many predict the world will warm between 1.8-3.6°F (2-4°C) by the year 2030, unless society reduces its output of greenhouse gases. These changes could endanger the existence of all life on Earth.

What Is the Greenhouse Effect?

Heat from the sun is being trapped inside the Earth's atmosphere by the "greenhouse" gases: carbon dioxide, methane and water vapor. These gases act like the windows of a greenhouse and trap heat in our atmosphere in a way that keeps the Earth at just the right temperature. If the Earth had no greenhouse gases in its air, most of the heat that it gets from the sun would escape into outer space and the Earth would be much colder than it is today.

Today, people are putting more and more greenhouse gases into the air, and more of the sun's heat is being trapped in our atmosphere.

Where Do Greenhouse Gases Come From?

Greenhouse gases are released when we burn coal, oil, wood or other fuel including those used to run our vehicles. Car and truck exhausts emit all kinds of pollutants, including nitrous oxide and lead, and vast quantities of the greenhouse gas carbon dioxide. Around the world greenhouse gases come from the methane from rice fields and rubbish dumps, aerosol sprays, refrigerator and air conditioner coolants and CFCs (chlorofluorocarbons).

Effects of Global Warming

Scientists are not quite sure how global warming will effect the world's weather but most believe that an increase in temperature of only a few degrees could be very dangerous to our planet and could cause:

- weather extremes
- crops to die and good crop-growing areas to become deserts
- many animals and plants to become extinct
- water shortages in some areas and too much rain in others
- the destruction of some forest areas before they expand to new growth areas
- the polar ice caps to melt adding enough water to the ocean to cause flooding in low-lying coastal areas

Save the Trees!

Large-scale destruction of forests may cause dangerous weather changes. Trees use lots of carbon dioxide and contribute to the delicate balance of gases that helps to keep our planet at the correct temperature. Fewer trees means more carbon dioxide in our atmosphere.

155

TLC10072 Copyright © Teaching & Learning Company, Carthage, IL 62321-0010

Ozone Depletion

High in the stratosphere is a thin layer of gas called ozone. The ozone layer absorbs more than 90% of the sun's harmful ultraviolet (burning) rays. In 1985, intense depletion of the ozone, called a hole, was discovered in the ozone layer over the Antarctic. At times, that hole was as big as the United States. Four years later a smaller hole was found over the Arctic and thinning was found in several places. Today, the ozone layer is continuing to thin over many large cities.

What's Happening to the Ozone Layer?

Our life-style is adversely affecting the ozone layer. Scientists studying the ozone layer think that it is being attacked by chemicals called chlorofluorocarbons (CFCs). These drift up high in the sky and turn ozone into ordinary oxygen. CFCs were recently used in aerosol spray cans and foam packaging but are now banned in the United States and Canada. CFCs are still used in refrigerators and air conditioners and in some packaging.

Holes in the Ozone Are a Pain in the Skin!

When people receive too much ultraviolet radiation, they suffer a bad sunburn and may develop skin cancer later in life. UV rays may be invisible, but their effects can be seen in sunburns, premature aging of the skin, skin cancer, cataracts of the eye, damage to sea creatures living near the water's surface and damage to crops. Let's hope we can protect the ozone layer–so it can protect us!

What's Being Done?

In 1987, 40 countries signed a treaty pledging to decrease the world's output of CFCs in half by 1994. In 1990, many countries agreed to stop using CFCs by the year 2000. Chemicals released in the past will remain in the atmosphere for a long time and will continue to deplete the ozone layer. When ozone-destroying pollutants are totally eliminated, it is hoped that the ozone layer will be able to replenish itself.

All living organisms contribute to the balance of gases in the troposphere. Oxygen comes mostly from plants. Plants absorb carbon dioxide and release oxygen. Animals, including people, inhale oxygen and exhale carbon dioxide. In fact, the respiration of animals and plants on land and in the oceans plays a big part in keeping the gases in the troposphere in balance.

Acid Rain

Rain is slightly acidic even in unpolluted air. The chemicals that make the air polluted sometimes cause the rain or snow to be more acidic than usual. This is called acid rain. Nowadays, rain that falls in North America and Europe is sometimes more acidic than lemon juice! We can't feel acid rain when it falls, but it does hurt our environment, which affects all living things.

Scientists believe the acid in rain comes from the burning of fossil fuels (car exhausts, factories) and the wastes from power stations. The burning of fossil fuels produces carbon dioxide, plus small amounts of nitrogen and sulphur dioxide. These gases mix with water vapor in clouds making a weak solution of nitric acid and sulfuric acid. Pollution from one city can become acid rain in another city. Laws are in place in some areas to enforce industries using coal or oil to put "scrubbers" on their chimneys to filter out harmful chemicals released in their smoke.

Acid rain is poisoning our water systems and the creatures that live in them; it is damaging our forests; attacking our crops and even destroying stonework on buildings, bridges and statues.

The acidity of rain is measured by its pH level. Pure rain has a pH level of 5.6. Acid rain is any rain with a pH level lower than 5.6. If too much acid rain falls into a lake, the lake may become acidified. Fish cannot survive with a pH level below 4.5.

How Much Acid Is in Your Rain?

Materials

red cabbage
lemon juice
rainwater
tap water
stove or burner
pot of boiling water
container
strainer
strips of white construction
    paper

What to Do

1 Boil half a red cabbage in water and let it soak for three hours.

2 Strain cabbage water into a container.

3 Soak the strips of construction paper in the cabbage water and lay them flat to dry.

4 Dip the dried strips into lemon juice, tap water and local rainwater.

5 These strips are your acid testers. The more acid in your liquid, the pinker your strip.

City Weather

Circle all of the things in this picture that pollute our planet and affect the weather. Color the picture.

Kids Can Help!

We are using up our natural resources at an alarming rate, so fast in fact that many of our animals and plants, and the places where they live, will disappear unless we change our ways. Although children cannot change the ways of society, they can be made aware of the consequences of their actions on the environment and adopt life-style changes that will make less of an impact on our environment. Their awareness alone might make a difference. It can be shared with their parents who in turn can make their own changes to save our world. Following are many ways that kids can help:

Spread the Environmental Message

- Inform yourself! Read up on it! Join a local environmental group.
- Inform others about how polluted our waters are and how important this water is to everything on Earth. Describe how our waters, land air are being used as dumping grounds for unnecessary waste products. Speak for the animals, fish, plants and humans and help to make others care about our life-sustaining Earth.
- Inform others about how we are using up the resources and contaminating our world.
- Spread the word about the products that are most harmful to our environment.
- Write letters to world leaders asking for laws to cut the pollution that causes acid rain and the greenhouse effect.

Save Energy

Conserve energy by turning off lights, televisions or computers when they are not in use.

Stop the Poisoning

Help with lawn and garden work so poison pesticides and chemical fertilizers will not be needed. Adopt the "weeds are beautiful" motto!

Help Reduce Greenhouse Gases in Our Air

Walk, cycle or carpool to school, activities or friends' homes. Encourage others to do the same.

Don't Buy It

- Refuse to buy products that are sold with excess packaging. Write to the companies about the unnecessary waste being created.
- Protect the ozone layer by boycotting foam packaging. Inform restaurants and grocery stores about your choices.
- Don't buy products that use rain forest timber, like television sets with rosewood panelling; souvenirs made from coral or seashells or clothing made from the skins of endangered animals.

Reuse and Recycle

- Inform others that each person in North America throws away about one ton (one tonne) of garbage every year, and we are running out of places to put it!
- Recycle your possessions and their packages. Pass items on to others. Host a garage sale.
- Do you recycle cardboard, paper products, plastics, tins, glass and compostable materials? Take on a class project to instigate such programs if they are not already in place.

Plan a Neighborhood Cleanup

Pitch it in . . . the garbage that is! Take a garbage bag for a walk around the school yard or neighborhood. Experience the sense of cooperative community and responsibility that comes with caring for your environment.

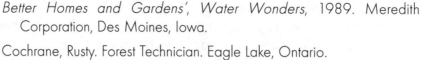

Resources

Better Homes and Gardens', *Water Wonders*, 1989. Meredith Corporation, Des Moines, Iowa.

Cochrane, Rusty. Forest Technician. Eagle Lake, Ontario.

Gibbons, Gail. *Weather Forecasting*. Macmillan, 1987.

Gibbons, Gail. *Weather Predictions*. Macmillan, 1987.

Henson, Collins M. *Your Environment: Air, Air Pollution, and Weather*. Interstate, 1971.

An Introduction to Weather. National Geographic, 1971.

Jennings, Gary. *Killer Storms: Hurricanes, Typhoons, and Tornadoes*. Lippincott, 1970.

Looking at Weather. David Suzuki with Barbara Hehner, Stoddart Young Readers, Stoddart, 1988, New Data Enterprises, Toronto.

McCauley, Terry. Interviews, classes and resources. Banting Memorial High School, Alliston, Ontario, 1977-81.

Palazzo, Janet. *What Makes the Weather?* Troll Associates, 1982.

Pollard, Michael. *Air, Water, and Weather*. Facts on File, 1987.

Sattler, Helen R. *Nature's Weather Forecasters*. Nelson, 1978.

The Science Book of Weather. Neil Ardley, Doubleday Canada Limited, Copyright 1992, Dorling Kindersley Limited, London.

Science in Elementary Education, 6th edition, Peter C. Gega, Macmillan Publishing Company, New York, 1990.

Watts, Alan. *Instant Weather Forecasting*. Dodd, 1968.

Weather, Eyewitness Book, 1991, Stoddart, Canada, Toronto, Brian Cosgrove.

Ontario Division
Canadian Cancer Society
1639 Yonge Street
Toronto, Ontario
Canada M4T 2W6
416-488-5400

Environment Canada
Place Vincent Massey
351 St. Joseph Blvd.
Hull, Quebec
Canada K1G 0H3
1-800-668-6767

At the time of publication, every effort was made to insure the accuracy of the information included in this book. However, we cannot guarantee that the agencies and organizations mentioned will continue to operate or to maintain these current locations.